D0916003

DISCARDED

Studies in
Writing & Rhetoric

IN 1980, THE CONFERENCE ON COLLEGE COMPOSITION AND COMmunication perceived a need for providing publishing opportunities for monographs that were too long for publication in its journal and too short for the typical scholarly books published by The National Council of Teachers of English. The Studies in Writing and Rhetoric series was conceived, and a Publications Committee established.

Monographs to be considered for publication may be speculative, theoretical, historical, analytical, or empirical studies; research reports; or other works contributing to a better understanding of composition and communication, including interdisciplinary studies or studies in related disciplines. The SWR series will exclude textbooks, unrevised dissertations, book-length manuscripts, course syllabi, lesson plans, and collections of previously published material.

Any teacher-writer interested in submitting a work for publication in this series should submit either a prospectus and sample manuscript or a full manuscript to the NCTE Director of Publications, 1111 Kenyon Road, Urbana, IL 61801. Accompanied by sample manuscript, a prospectus should contain a rationale, a definition of readership within the CCCC constituency, comparison with related extant publications, a tentative table of contents, and an estimate of length in double-spaced 8½ × 11 sheets and the date by which full manuscript can be expected. Manuscripts should be in the range of 100 to 170 typed manuscript pages.

The present work serves as a model for future SWR monographs.

Paul O'Dea
NCTE Director of Publications

COLLEGE OF THE SEQUOIAS
LIBRARY

Writer's Block: The Cognitive Dimension

Mike Rose

WITH A FOREWORD BY MARILYN S. STERNGLASS

Published for Conference on College
Composition and Communication

SOUTHERN ILLINOIS UNIVERSITY PRESS
Carbondale and Edwardsville

COLLEGE OF THE SEQUOIAS
LIBRARY

Production of works in this series has been partly funded by the Conference on College Composition and Communication of the National Council of Teachers of English.

Copyright © 1984 by Conference on College Composition and Communication

All rights reserved

Printed in the United States of America
Designed by Design for Publishing, Inc., Bob Nance
Production supervised by John DeBacher

89 88 87   4 3 2

Library of Congress Cataloging in Publication Data

Rose, Mike.
   Writer's block.

   (Studies in writing and rhetoric)
   Bibliography: p.
   1. Writer's block.   2. Creative writing—Psychological
aspects.   3. Creation (Literary, artistic, etc.)
I. Title.   II. Series.
BF456.W8R67   1984   808'.001'9   83-662
ISBN 0-8093-1141-0

To
my Mother
and
the memory of my Father

the quiet love
the courage

Contents

Illustrations

Tables

Figure

Foreword

Marilyn S. Sternglass

CURRENT RESEARCH IN THE COMPOSING PROCESS ENCOUR-ages us to believe that if we expose our students to process-centered strategies, allow them ample time for invention procedures, the writing of multiple drafts, real audience feedback, and delayed attention to editing, we will have solved most of our instructional problems. Students who fail to produce competent prose under these conditions are either too poorly motivated or too incompetent to succeed. Now Mike Rose has come along with a study of the cognitive dimension of writer's block that neatly punctures our self-satisfied stance and forces us to reexamine some of our newly won, highly cherished assumptions.

Students who are shown to be neither incompetent nor unmotivated demonstrate ineffective strategies when trying to address complex tasks, and in this important study Mike Rose describes, analyzes, and finally explains the causes of their difficulties. He begins by postulating six basic reasons why some students manifest blocking characteristics when confronting a complex writing task: rigid rules, misleading assumptions about composing, premature editing, poor or inappropriate planning, conflicting rules or strategies, and inadequately understood evaluative criteria.

Rose also leads us to examine recent speculation about how writing is produced. Current models present composing as a primarily hierarchical process during which writers tend to move from broad goal-oriented concerns to the production of specific sentences. This "top-down" orientation is meant to be a corrective to earlier "bottom-up" approaches that had students working from word to phrase to sentence to paragraph. But rather than either of these approaches, Rose offers a model of opportunism which suggests that while writers sometimes operate hierarchically, they also respond in less orderly fashion to emerging linguistic and rhetorical possibilities.

Three purposes dominate Rose's study of the causes of writer's block: (1) the development of a questionnaire to identify blockers; (2) the selection, observation, and stimulated-recall examination of students experiencing high and low degrees of blocking; (3) a preliminary proposal of a model of composing. The questionnaire contained 24 items, and from its analysis Rose concluded that it offered "confirmation of the study's assumption that a considerable dimension of writer's block involves cognitive/behavioral and cognitive/attitudinal variables." For teachers puzzled by the writing behavior of seemingly competent students, the questionnaire can provide valuable insights into the attitudes, strategies, and processes used by their students. The stimulated-recall methodology used by Rose to prompt the students' remembrance of their thoughts while composing consisted of viewing videotapes of the writing activities with the writers immediately after they had completed their composing. Rose felt that composing aloud, as in other protocol studies, would have interfered with their normal composing behaviors. Through these investigations and with the analyses of the texts that were produced, Rose was able to propose a preliminary model of composing. Central to this model is that writers must possess a repertoire of "strategies, rules, plans, frames, and possibly, evaluative criteria, and the richer the repertoire, the richer the opportunistic activity."

Through the case studies presented in this study, Rose explores the strategies and processes of two students, one a high-blocker and one a low-blocker. These detailed descriptions bring alive the processes and problems being explored and demonstrate vividly how complex approaching a writing task is. Mike Rose's analysis of these problems, his proposed model of composing, and his implications for teachers of writing constitute important contributions to our understanding of another dimension of the complex process of writing.

Bloomington, Indiana
January 1983

Preface

THIS STUDY BEGAN FROM A HAPPY COINCIDENCE OF PUBLIC work and private reading. I was teaching Introduction to Literature at the same time I was browsing through the fascinating and, by now, somewhat exotic work of the classical Gestalt psychologists. The browsing was sparking an interest in what these days is called cognitive psychology or cognitive science—a sometimes reductive but sometimes illuminating study of the way we deal with information and solve problems. As it turned out, my private reading would follow this direction over the next few years. As for my public work, the teaching was, as it always had been, a pleasure. I had the usual group of students: those whose comments revealed a bright eagerness, others whose remarks bespoke of premature cynicism. And their papers displayed a familiar range as well: quick and superficial to cautious and penetrating. We've all seen this range of quality. And, we've all heard the sorts of things the students were telling me about these papers during conferences. This time, though, my night reading sensitized me to something I had certainly seen (and heard) before but had not really quite *seen*: the degree to which certain kinds of planning strategies and rules about writing were interfering with some of my students' composing.

My recognition led to several pilot studies, one of which I wrote up in an essay entitled "Rigid Rules, Inflexible Plans, and the Stifling of Language." I sent the essay forth and it was energetically sent back enough times to make me doubt the utility of matching cognitive psychology and stymied composing. But the essay finally found a home in the December 1980 issue of *College Composition and Communication* and the acceptance encouraged me to conduct subsequent studies which, however, had to be both cautious and complex, for the speculations in "Rigid Rules" were very much the result of simple investigations. It is these subsequent studies—ranging over several years and involving just over one thousand students—that I offer to the reader of the present volume. But I don't want simply to report results. I want, as well, to offer the framework that informed the research.

Though cognitive psychology, like any psychology, can become narrow and philosophically constraining, it can also illuminate certain dimensions of the writing process, for it—the best of it anyway—explores the ways we carry out plans and strategies, organize information, and evaluate what we do. Much of the present volume (and of "Rigid Rules" as well) provides a kind of introduction to this particular way of thinking about thinking. In applying the cognitive perspective to writing, I have tried to avoid its esoterica and jargon, but there is a point past which the abandonment of terminology and the trimming away of procedures result in the trivializing of a discipline. Thus, some special terms remain, but their meaning will be clarified by context, and where this is not the case, I have defined them with appositives or parenthetical phrases.

I offer this cognitive framework not out of evangelical zeal. My own psychological training falls more in the psychodynamic/psychoanalytic camp. But the psychodynamic approach seemed to have limited explanatory power for most of the students I studied closely. Frameworks (or models or paradigms) are like the lenses in a Phoroptor, the machine optometrists use to determine the effects different lenses have on vision. Switch lenses and different aspects of a phenomenon will come into focus. We'll see clearly what was once fuzzy or indistinct. In my case, the cognitive framework brought into resolve what had heretofore been hazy. But an aphorism of Kenneth Burke's must be kept in mind: "A way of seeing is also a way of not seeing." Any framework excludes as well as includes. The present study attempts to highlight a particular dimension of writer's block; it does not attempt a comprehensive treatment of a highly complex problem. As I note in the Afterword, there are a number of psychodynamic and sociological issues that remain for others to explore. However, if I am right in my investigations of and judgments about the cognitive dimension of writer's block, then this study's findings are of great importance to teachers. If a student's reliance on rigid rules, inflexible plans, narrow assumptions and evaluative criteria is not rooted in some complex emotional reality or in an intractable social context, then teachers and tutors can readily intervene. Cognitive problems are vulnerable to teaching and reteaching, conferencing, modeling. Furthermore, an investigation of cognitive problems can also have implications for the teaching of writing in general—for the teaching of grammar and stylistic rules, planning strategies, and the nature of composing. The last section of the Conclusion chapter is devoted to speculations about this study's implications for instruction.

A good deal of the work I'm about to report was originally written up as a doctoral dissertation. At points throughout the present volume I refer the research-oriented reader to that dissertation. But the present volume is self-contained and includes research that I conducted after the completion of the dissertation, as well as some rethinking of older formulations and development of new perspectives.

A number of people provided assistance during the writing of the dissertation, and I thank them in that volume. Some of those people, however, were particularly instrumental in the conceiving and execution of my work and I continue to draw upon their intelligence and their kindness. Richard Shavelson, a first-rate methodologist, chaired my dissertation committee and has become a kind of academic crisis counselor, only a phone call away to protect me from my own statistical illiteracy. Ruth Mitchell is my other mentor. Her advice is always generous and penetrating. Many thanks are also due Noreen Webb and Barbara Hayes-Roth who provided a good deal of help with statistical analysis and model-building. I must also acknowledge the masterful work of Chris Myers, my programmer, and the selflessness of Nancy Sommers, who read and carefully commented on the dissertation. Finally, there are people who were particularly helpful at the beginning and the end of this journey: James Britton encouraged me when I figured that "Rigid Rules" was fit for files only, and Lee Odell provided a thorough review of an earlier version of the present manuscript.

Some typists transport words mindlessly from page, through fingertips, onto page; others read carefully, edit, and comment graciously. Antonia Turman represents the best of the second breed. I, and many, many others, owe her a great deal of thanks.

Writer's Block

1

Introduction

"YOU DON'T KNOW WHAT IT IS," WROTE FLAUBERT, "TO STAY A whole day with your head in your hands trying to squeeze your unfortunate brain so as to find a word." Though histrionic, Flaubert's complaint is all too familiar to professional writers, student writers, and teachers of writing. Henry Miller was never able to complete his book on Lawrence; certain of our students flounder across deadlines; some of us have stalled on memos and reports as the blank page gleamed. Unfortunately, researchers have no surveys or tabulations of how many writers—professional or student—experience writer's block. But autobiographical and biographical material reveals that even the greatest of writers—from Melville to Forster to Styron—have been stymied. My pilot surveys suggest that at least 10 percent of college students block frequently, and the boom of "writer's block" workshops stands as a reminder that writer's block is a problem outside of the classroom as well.[1] And the problem might not simply be one of discomfort and missed deadlines. Extrapolating from Morris Holland's report on the related problem of writing anxiety,[2] it is possible that sustained experiences of writer's block influence students' career choices. Frequent blockers could have trouble envisioning themselves in jobs requiring reports or extensive memoranda.

The odd thing is that though writer's block is a familiar, even popular notion, it is one of the least studied dysfunctions of the composing process. Skill problems have long been examined and a bewildering panoply of treatments—from sentence-combining to role-playing—has been built. But when the *capable* writer cannot write, we are puzzled and often resort to broad affective explanations, e.g., "He's afraid of evaluation," "She's too hard on herself." Significantly, the one possibly related topic that does appear in the research literature is "writing apprehension" or "writing anxiety"—again, affective. It is possible that this affective bent explains why writer's block has never been the object of the educator's scrutiny: it is perceived as a mysterious, amorphous emotional difficulty, not as a delimitable problem that can be analyzed and then remedied through instruction and tutorial programs. Before one can hope, then, to help people through writer's block, the basic questions have to be answered—what is writer's block and what causes it? Then the applied, more practical stage of such investigation can emerge: how can one help students, businessmen, even professional writers unlock their unfortunate brains to start the flow of words once again?

But delimiting and defining a notion as complex and tinged with myth and popular speculation as writer's block is more easily said than done. How can writer's block become the focus of careful study? Two initial procedures are necessary: (1) A definition must be proposed that posits exclusion rules, that is, establishes boundaries for rejecting inappropriate cases. (2) Patterns must be sought out in whatever data are available; then suitable models can be proposed—the legitimacy of a particular model being determined by its capacity to explain the data. Further, more rigorous studies can then be conducted to test the model. Considering writer's block, several models come to mind: behaviorist (to explore histories of unpleasant writing experience), psychoanalytic (to explore deep-seated fears and defenses), and sociological/political (to explore the environmental conditions that limit a writer). My preliminary explorations, some of which are presented in "Rigid Rules, Inflexible Plans, and the Stifling of Language: A Cognitivist Analysis of Writer's Block," suggested that narrow or inappropriate composing rules and planning strategies could be confounding student writers.[3] Therefore, the model afforded by cognitive psychology seemed a suitable framework with which to explain the data. The present study will also bring that model to bear on writer's block. My assumption is that some cases of students' writer's block might be linked to variables that are more cognitive than affective or motivational (though there might be affective and motivational corollaries to and consequences of the cognitive), and more cognitive than sociological/political (though there could be a sociological/political dimension to the writing situations in which rules, plans, and other cognitive operations are enacted). To my knowledge, a cognitive orientation has never been applied to writer's block, and thus that dimension of blocking has not been examined and described. But even with the limited focus the cognitive paradigm affords, the present study sprawls. Writer's block is an exceptionally complicated phenomenon.

Definition of Writer's Block

First, I'll establish delimiting boundaries.

1. Certainly, the basic writer (e.g., as described by Mina Shaughnessy and by Sondra Perl)[4] has difficulty getting words on paper. But, though sociolinguistic and affective forces interfere, a major reason for these students' scant productions is simply a lack of fundamental writing skills. The first clarifying boundary that must be established is that blocking presupposes basic writing skills that, for some reason, cannot be exercised.

2. A student can possess basic skills but still not produce much because she is tired, bored, or, in some way, not committed to completing the writing task at hand. But one could not speak of blocking here, for the student's skills are not truly brought into play. The second boundary is that blocking presupposes some degree of alertness and of effort.

Writer's block, then, can be defined as an inability to begin or continue writing for reasons other than a lack of basic skill or commitment. Blocking is not simply measured by the passage of time (for writers often spend productive time toying with ideas without putting pen to paper), but by the passage of time with limited productive involvement in the writing task. Certain behaviors (i.e., missing deadlines) are associated with blocking. Feelings of anxiety, frustration, anger, or confusion often characterize this unproductive work. Blocking can be manifested in a variety of ways: some high-blockers produce only a few sentences; others produce many more, but these sentences will be false starts, repetitions, blind alleys, or disconnected fragments of discourse; still others produce a certain amount of satisfactory prose only to stop in mid-essay. But since blocking is a composing process dysfunction that is related to skill in complex, not simple, ways, some high-blockers might eventually produce quality papers.

How does writer's block differ from the related concept of writing apprehension? As defined here, writer's block is broader and subsumes writing apprehension as a possible cause of or reaction to blocking. My preliminary case-study investigations suggest that not all high-blockers are apprehensive about writing (though they might get momentarily anxious when deadlines loom). For that fact, high-blockers do not necessarily share the characteristics attributed by John Daly and his associates to writing-apprehensive students: avoidance of courses and majors involving writing and lower skills as measured by objective and essay tests.[5] In addition, not all low-blockers fit Lynn Bloom's observation that nonanxious writers find writing enjoyable and seek out opportunities to practice it.[6] Apprehensiveness, then, can lead to blocking (the anxiety being caused by prior negative evaluations[7] or by more complex psychodynamics[8]) or can result from the fix blockers find themselves in. But blocking and apprehensiveness (and low-blocking and nonapprehensiveness) are not synonymous, not necessarily coexistent, and not necessarily causally linked.

As I've suggested, there can be a number of affective and motivational explanations for why writers get stymied, but the present study will attempt to illuminate primarily cognitive variables involved in writer's block. Some writers block for one or more of the following reasons: (1) the rules by which they guide their composing processes are rigid, inappropriately invoked, or incorrect; (2) their assumptions about composing are misleading; (3) they edit too early in the composing process; (4) they lack appropriate planning and discourse strategies or rely on inflexible or inappropriate strategies; (5) they invoke conflicting rules, assumptions, plans, and strategies; and (6) they evaluate their writing with inappropriate criteria or criteria that are inadequately understood.

A number of terms used in the above discussion need to be more fully defined.

Definition of Terms

Rule: A composing rule is a linguistic, sociolinguistic, formal, or process directive (e.g., "When possible, avoid the passive voice," or "If you can't get started, try freewriting").

Rigid, Inappropriately Invoked, or Incorrect Rules: A rigid rule is one that dictates absolutes in areas where context and purpose should direct behavior (e.g., "Always put your thesis statement at the end of your first paragraph," or "Never use the verb 'to be'"). An inappropriate rule is a normally legitimate directive invoked at a questionable time and place in the composing process (e.g., "The length of sentences should be varied," invoked during rough drafting). An incorrect rule is one that is simply not true (e.g., "It is wrong to begin a sentence with 'And'").

Composing-Process Assumptions and Misleading Assumptions: A composing-process assumption is any belief about the way writing occurs. A misleading assumption is a belief that does not reflect the diversity and complexity of the composing process (e.g., "The best writing comes with little toil; it is inspired and flows onto the page").

Premature Editing: Editing is defined as the minor revising that attends to the surface of language: mechanical/grammatical, spelling, lexical, syntactical inaccuracies and inconsistencies are corrected and semantic/syntactic preferences—usually at the sentence level—are enacted. Though it is fallacious to assume that content and verbal surface are neatly separable, these corrections and alterations often do not reflect a writing rethinking, but, rather, a writer tidying up. Editing becomes anti-productive and premature when the writer unduly attends to mechanical/verbal surface while roughing out ideas or writing a first draft. She is refining surface instead of testing ideas and thinking freely.

Interpretive and Writing Strategies for Complexity: This broad category subsumes the variety of interpretive, planning, and writing strategies a student brings to bear on university writing tasks. These tasks, usually higher-level exposition (e.g., classification, compare/contrast, analysis) and argument, demand of the student what James Moffett has labeled generalizing and theorizing.[9] The tasks do not call for the simple chronological pattern found in narration or for the spatial, object-referenced structure of description; rather, students have to rely on more abstract frameworks. And while a number of university students can produce a relatively error-free prose and can write description and narration well enough, higher-level exposition and argument often stump them.[10] The reasons they're stumped are both cognitive and linguistic, that is, involve both conceiving and planning material as well as generating and shaping written language.[11]

Problems can arise before actual writing is attempted. The way a student goes about *interpreting* the material from which she must work might be ineffective. For example, she might fail to highlight pertinent information in lengthy materials, or, conversely, might get so embroiled in dissecting materials that she produces an over-whelming, and possibly undifferentiated, array of information.

Related to interpretive strategies (and to discourse frames) are the *planning* strategies students bring to bear on composing. A fundamental assumption of this study is that since school-based writing is obviously nonrandom, purposive behavior, students bring guiding strategies to the production of discourse. These strategies or plans can be as formal as an outline or as unspecific and "rhythmic" as a movement from thesis to evidence to solution. A student, either on paper or in her head, can plot out the specifics of her strategy before beginning or in increments as she produces her essay. Whatever the case, some plans can prove to be dysfunctional: an inflexible plan is one that does not allow modification or alternatives. An inappropriate plan is a normally functional strategy used at the wrong place or time in the composing process. Individual differences are involved here, but one example could be the construction of a detailed outline for a piece of expressive prose. A subcategory of the inappropriate plan is the inadequate plan—a strategy too simple for the task at hand, e.g., a linear, chronological approach to a compare/contrast assignment.

As for *writing*, students might lack the ability to produce and manipulate the frames of discourse that are required in academic writing. They might also lack a repertoire of inter- and intra-paragraph cohesive ties[12]—particularly transitional devices—or rhetorical strategies necessary to establish complex relations among ideas. They might, as well, lack the wide range of sentence-level syntactic options needed to represent the ideational complexities they wish to articulate.[13] The discussion here is obviously of specific higher-order skills related to specific writing situations. But the underdevelopment of these skills can stymie the exercise of a student's more general competence.

Conflict: Conflict is defined as a cognitive discord between rules, strategies, or assumptions. A writer writes with the rapid play of numerous rules, strategies, and assumptions, but there are times when they work against each other. An illustration: "Avoid the passive voice" coupled with "Keep the 'I' out of reports." If the writer does not possess some criteria by which she can give one rule more weight than another as the situation demands, she will find herself stuck at a number of junctures in her composing.

Attitudes toward Writing: An attitude is an "evaluative orientation"[14] toward, in this case, the act or result of composing. Attitudes toward writing are most likely formed by one's history of evaluation by others[15] and are reflected in the evaluations a student levels at or imagines others leveling at his work. These evaluations can be broad ("This paper is no good") or specific ("My conclusion seems tacked-on"). An assumption of this study is that evaluation is rooted in a comparison with internalized criteria of good writing and/or with beliefs about the criteria other audiences will use. Evaluation becomes inappropriate when the criteria a student has internalized and/or attributes to others are overblown or inadequately understood.

Notes Toward a Cognitive Model of the Composing Process

Terms have been defined but have not been organized in a way that illustrates their relation to each other. A model could best provide this illustration, but since I have not conducted the extensive studies necessary to validate a comprehensive model of the composing process, what follows must be read as speculation.

To date, only a handful of researchers have presented models of the composing process that are based on cognitive psychology: Bertram Bruce, Allan Collins, and Ann Rubin in "A Cognitive Science Approach to Writing"; Ellen Nold in "Revising"; and Linda Flower and John Hayes in *A Process Model of Composition.*[16]

Though Bruce and his associates and Nold offer theoretically rich models, both have limitations. Bruce et al., working from "cognitive science and hence, historically, from theoretical linguistics and artificial intelligence" (p. 3), admit that the composing sequences they propose "are not carried out in the strict order implied" (p. 12) in their article, but continue to represent writing as a hierarchical, successively elaborated process. An example: "Let us think, then, of writing as a procedure with two major steps, which are temporally ordered: 1) generating ideas; 2) generating structure" (p. 7). Relying on a cognitive/developmental orientation, Nold criticizes linear models of composing and considers individual differences in writers and tasks in constructing her own model. Yet though she grounds her discussion on George Miller's general principles of allotment of cognitive resources, she focuses her essay on revision, and thus, of necessity, does not provide a comprehensive model of all dimensions of composing.

In *A Process Model*, Flower and Hayes have constructed an empirically based model of composing that accounts for the writer's memory, a variety of the writer's composing subprocesses, and the materials outside the writer including the product he's producing. The model is based on and reflects at least five fundamental precepts: "Writing is goal directed"; "Writing processes are hierarchically organized"; "Some writing processes may interrupt other processes over which they have priority"; "Writing processes may be organized recursively"; "Writing goals may be modified as writing proceeds" (pp. 95–97). Flower and Hayes' is the most detailed, multioperational, and comprehensive of composing models constructed to date. However, one important quality of the model restricts its fluidity (or requires the positing of overly complex operations to maintain fluidity). Possibly following the pioneering work on planning conducted by George Miller, Eugene Galanter, and Karl Pribram,[17] Flower and Hayes developed their model from a "top-down," hierarchically deductive perspective, so that the fundamental orientation is to view the writer as working in orderly fashion from, say, generation of ideas to production of sentences. Flower and Hayes admit that not all writing proceeds in so neat a fashion and pose the mathematical concept of "recursiveness" to allow for a "complex intermingling of stages" (p. 46). They pose, as well, the notion of "priority interrupts," a process by which editing can "take precedence over all other writing processes in the sense that editing may interrupt the other processes at any time" (p. 99). After editing, "the generating [of new ideas] process appears to be second in order of precedence since it interrupts any process except editing" (p. 99). Perhaps these very important operations of "recursiveness" and "priority interrupts" could be accounted for in a less mechanical way—the mechanical orderliness of Flower and Hayes' rendering possibly being rooted in the hierarchical model of Miller and his associates, and, too, in Flower and Hayes' method of gathering data (having writers speak aloud while composing). It is conceivable that when a writer speaks as he writes, he articulates a more ordered flow of thought than would naturally occur.

I believe that the operations implied in "recursiveness" and "priority interrupts" can better be represented by what Barbara and Frederick Hayes-Roth have labeled "opportunism."[18] Though their work deals with the planning process, the Hayes-Roths' fundamental assumptions are applicable to writing, for some form and level of planning and enacting are central to the composing process.

The Hayes-Roths explain opportunism thus:

> We assume that people's planning activity is largely *opportunistic*. That is, at each point in the process, the planner's current decisions and observations suggest various opportunities for plan development. The planner's subsequent decisions follow up on selected opportunities. Sometimes, these decision-sequences follow an orderly path and produce a neat top-down expansion. . . . However, some decisions and observations might also suggest less orderly opportunities for plan development. . . .
>
> This view of the planning process suggests that planners will produce many coherent decision sequences, but less coherent sequences as well. In extreme cases, the overall process might appear chaotic. The relative orderliness of particular planning processes presumably reflects individual differences among planners as well as different task demands. (p. 276)

Applied to writing, opportunism suggests that the goals, plans, discourse frames, and information that emerge as a writer confronts a task are not always hierarchically sequenced from most general strategy to most specific activity. These goals, plans, frames, etc., can influence each other in a rich variety of ways; for example, while editing a paragraph, a writer may see that material can be organized in a different way or as a writer writes a certain phrase, it could cue other information stored in memory. This fundamental reciprocity between intent and discovery, goal orientation and goal modification is anecdotally documented by professional writers,[19] and the notion of opportunism provides a cognitive science operation to account for it.

The scheme I'm about to present owes a great deal to Flower and Hayes' elucidation in *A Process Model* of writing subprocesses and to the Hayes-Roths' notion of opportunism. But what follows is by no means a comprehensive model of the composing process. In fact, it is more a hypothesis preliminary to model-building, a metaphorical representation that highlights several key dimensions and functions of the composing process relevant to the present study: the relation of writing to high-level strategies and general problem-solving/composing orientations, and to rules, plans, and discourse frames.

A writer comes to a writing task with *domain knowledge*, that is, with facts and propositions about myriad topics stored in long-term memory. Some of this knowledge will be retrieved for composing. (This knowledge can also be stored in nonlinguistic fashion—tacitly, imagistically.)

The writer also brings with him a number of *composing subprocesses*. These are linguistic, stylistic, rhetorical, sociolinguistic, and process rules, interpretive as well as intersentence to discourse-level writing plans, discourse frames, and attitudes, all of which select, shape, organize, and evaluate domain knowledge. Though there are numerous rules, plans, and discourse frames, they can be categorized as being either flexible and multioptional or one-directional, rigid, inflexible. A particularly important composing activity is "shaping" which occurs as domain knowledge—propositions, even images—is converted to written language. (James Britton calls the particular moment of conversion of mind to page "shaping at the point of utterance."[20]) Editing occurs when the writer focuses on the correction or refinement of language already rehearsed in mind or written on paper. Attitudes are manifested when writers evaluate what they've written.

Directing the writer's subprocesses are *executive operations*. These high-level, often assumption-based, strategies select, organize, and activate composing subprocesses. It is possible that these strategies themselves are conceived of, organized, or weighted in ways that account for general problem-solving or composing styles.

Outside of the writer is the *task environment*, which includes a particular writing project, all attendant materials, and the words-on-page the writer has converted from thought to written language.[21]

As was stated earlier, some cognitive models posit "top-down," deductive, successively elaborated problem-solving behavior. For example, at the extreme, a writer chooses an executive-level strategy (e.g., "I'll make this paper an argument") which, in turn, determines the selection and focusing of composing subprocesses which, further, organize and shape domain knowledge. Much less common are cognitive models that stress "bottom-up," inductive, specific to general problem-solving behavior.[22] An extreme example of bottom-up composing behavior would be a writer toying with words and phrases until he develops, upward, an executive-level strategy for organizing his essay.

But this continual distinction between top-down and bottom-up behavior—at least as far as composing is concerned—is misleading. Even superficial examination of writers at work reveals the enactment, even the transaction, of both orientations. To posit one or the other as being the norm (or both as being the only possibilities) is to reduce the complexity of composing. Thus the notion of opportunism—with its emphasis on shifting between top-down and bottom-up behavior and shifting, as well, "horizontally" among executive operations, composing subprocesses, dimensions of knowledge, and elements of the task environment—seems much truer to the way writers write.

Blocking can occur if assumptions, strategies, or certain kinds of rules, plans, and frames hold a writer too rigidly to a top-down or bottom-up orientation or in some other way restrict opportunistic play. Blocking can also occur if the writer's assumptions, rules, etc., conflict or if the criteria to which he matches his production are inappropriate or inadequate. A schematic representation of selected aspects of the above discussion is presented in Figure 1.

Previous Studies of Writer's Block

I have attempted a definition of writer's block and have outlined a cognitive orientation with which to examine it. Before turning to the specifics of the study that was informed by this orientation, let me quickly survey previous work on writer's block. Unfortunately, there is not a great deal to summarize. I ran computer searches of *Psychological Abstracts, Dissertation Abstracts*, and ERIC and found no formal social science/educational investigations.[23]

The only piece of literary scholarship on writer's block is Tillie Olsen's *Silences*.[24] It approaches the problem from a sociological, primarily feminist perspective, anecdotally and often poetically de-

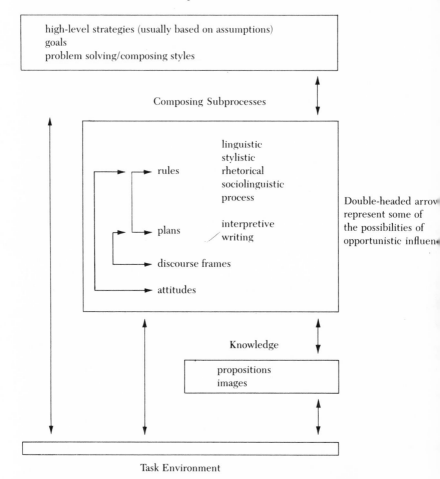

Fig. 1. A schematic representation of selected cognitive
dimensions and functions of the composing process.

tailing the dilemma of the writer stymied by an uncaring society. One can also find useful literary snippets in biographical and autobiographical sources and in interviews. A good contemporary resource is the four-volume *Paris Review* series *Writers at Work*.[25]

My survey of the literature on creativity revealed little. That literature, a good deal of which is based on psychoanalysis or Helmholtz/Wallas stage theories (e.g., preparation, incubation, illumination, verification), mostly deals with the functional creative process.

Psychoanalytic literature contains a fair amount of discussion of creative blocks, but surprisingly little concerns writing. Paul Federn analyzes what he refers to as "the neurotic style," but that is more a faulty style (with the faults suggesting psychological disturbances) than a blocked style.[26] In *Neurotic Distortions of the Creative Process*, Lawrence Kubie presents several cases of writers whose neuroses stymied their flow of prose, but their cases are so idiosyncratic that few generalizations can be drawn.[27] Though not a psychoanalyst, Marvin Rosenberg adapts a psychoanalytic framework to explore writer's block in playwrights. He suggests that people experiencing writer's block have been culturally conditioned to inhibit primary process fantasies and reports the successful use of hypnosis to release the creative imagination.[28] But the most prolific of psychoanalytic theorists on writer's block is Edmund Bergler. Bergler analyzed blocking in highly psychosexual terms, defining creative writing as an expression of unconscious defenses against oral-masochistic conflicts, and writer's block as the result of the breakdown of those defenses.[29]

A nonpsychoanalytic, psychodynamic interpretation of writer's block is offered by Paul Goodman. He sees the difficulty as lying in an author's inability to dissociate relationships and events (that could become the stuff of fiction) from the emotional reality of his or her own life.[30]

Writing textbooks could offer discussions of blocking. I reviewed 20 recently published or revised texts.[31] Texts that were based on Aristotelian rhetoric (and thus dealt with invention) or on currently popular prewriting notions detailed methods of generating ideas, but blocking itself was rarely discussed. Only one book (Frederick Crews' *The Random House Handbook*) directly addressed writer's block.

I did find two popular, self-help books on writer's block: Karin

Mack and Eric Skjei's *Overcoming Writing Blocks* and Joan Minninger's *Free Yourself to Write*.[32] *Overcoming Writing Blocks* presents a sensible blend of literary investigation and self-help psychology. The authors discuss and attempt to remedy the "resistances to self-exposure," "censorious inner critics," and misunderstandings of the composing process that they believe lead to blocking. *Free Yourself to Write* lays blame on teachers who scrutinized grammatical errors rather than the substance of student papers and on myths about writing (e.g., "You must be mad to write," "You must think before you write"). Since Minninger informs her book with a transactional analysis framework, she posits that these comments and myths restrict the child (the feeling dimension of personality) within us. Though Minninger provides guides to get the blocked writer started, she also questionably insists that writing is fun and that quality prose rests within each of us waiting to be released on the page.

A small body of literature exists for a phenomenon related to writer's block: writing apprehension or anxiety. That literature can further be separated into the questionnaire and correlational studies of John Daly and his associates and of Morris Holland, and the naturalistic studies of Lynn Bloom.[33] Daly defines writing apprehension as "a general avoidance of writing and situations perceived by the individual to potentially require some amount of writing accompanied by the potential for evaluation of that writing."[34] And Daly and Miller designed a 26-item, primarily attitudinal, questionnaire by which writing-apprehensive students can be identified. Through further questionnaire and correlational studies, Daly has suggested that writing-apprehensive students "not only write differently and with lower quality than low apprehensives, but, in addition, fail to demonstrate as strong a working knowledge of writing skills as low apprehensives."[35] When compared to low apprehensives, writing-apprehensive students also tend to have lower verbal SAT scores and to avoid classes, majors, and even occupations that require writing.

Holland developed a questionnaire somewhat like Daly and Miller's. He found that writing anxiety significantly correlates with avoidance of English classes and classes requiring papers, with number of books read per quarter, English classes taken in high school, grades in high school and college English classes, and with major and intended career.

Although Bloom relies on Daly and Miller's questionnaire as one means of identifying writing-anxious students, her studies do not present analyses of questionnaire (or correlational) data, but, rather, case-study material, and the subjects of these investigations, unlike those lower-division students in the bulk of Daly's work, range from freshmen to graduate students. Contra Daly and his associates, Bloom finds that some of her anxious writers are, in fact, good writers and do not necessarily steer clear of courses and majors that involve writing. Like their less skilled but equally anxious peers, however, they evince certain misconceptions (e.g., that others write better and with more ease than they do) and characteristics (e.g., perfectionism, procrastination). Nonanxious writers, on the other hand, tend to be realistic in their assessment of their writing and efficient in the management of their time.

To my knowledge, then, the only empirically based, systematic investigation of writer's block (vs. writing apprehension or writing anxiety) is "Rigid Rules, Inflexible Plans, and the Stifling of Language: A Cognitivist Analysis of Writer's Block." "Rigid Rules" presents the results of interviews with 10 UCLA undergraduates (five high-blockers and five low-blockers[36]). The interviews, admittedly more clinical than rigorously structured, focused on each student's composing process. Questions were based on notes, drafts, and finished products.

It turned out that students who were blocking seemed to be depending on rules or plans that were inflexible and thus inappropriate for a complex process like composing. Some examples: Ruth believed that every sentence she wrote had to come out grammatically correct the first time around. This rule led Ruth to edit before she wrote; it closed off the free flow of ideas that can be tidied up in later drafts. Martha created a plan of such elaborate complexity that she was unable to convert its elements into a short, direct essay. Her days were spent constructing a plan that looked like a diagram of protein synthesis (she was a Biology major), leaving her only hours to move from outline to paper to deadline. Mike anticipated assignments. He generated strategies and plans for probable paper topics or essay exam questions before they hit his desk. When his predictions were accurate, he did very well ("psyched-out" the professor), but when he was off, he had great difficulty changing his plans. Plans, for Mike, were exact structural and substantive blueprints, not fluid strategies with alternatives. And because Mike's plans were so inflexible, he blocked.

Low-blockers possessed rules as well. But their rules were expressed less absolutely ("Try to keep audience in mind") or contained more built-in alternatives ("I can use as many ideas in my thesis paragraph as I need, and then develop paragraphs for each idea"). The few absolute rules low-blockers did possess were admirably functional—e.g., "When stuck, write!" As for plans, low-blockers seemed to compose with fluid, flexible strategies. Susan, for example, described a general "mental outline" she followed but explained how, when stymied, she tried to conceptualize the assignment in different ways. The interesting thing is that low-blockers often described their planning strategies more vaguely than did high-blockers. It is possible—though a hunch—that this lack of precision masks complex strategies rich with alternatives.

I explored the above data via a cognitive framework, suggesting that the rich literature on planning and heuristic rules could be applied to, and illuminate, some instances of writer's block. As was implied earlier, writer's block could result when heuristic rules ("rules of thumb"), like "to grab your audience try writing a catchy opening," become absolutes, or when rules are invoked inappropriately (e.g., "write grammatically" during a first draft), or when planning strategies become rigid (e.g., Mike's anticipatory, all-or-nothing outlines). These are not primarily emotional difficulties; they are cognitive blunders and are thus clarified through cognitive psychology's conceptual lens.

Overview of the Present Study

During the first phase of the present study, I developed a questionnaire with which to identify students experiencing writer's block. The questionnaire contains items that describe blocking behaviors and items that describe cognitive and cognitive/attitudinal variables related to blocking. The behavioral items allow one to quickly identify students experiencing writer's block. The additional items assist in identification of blockers and, as well, enable one to diagnose certain cognitive and cognitive/attitudinal difficulties.

During the second phase of the study, I selected 10 students who scored high and low on various combinations of the questionnaire's behavioral, cognitive, and attitudinal items. Each of the 10 students was videotaped while writing on a university-level expository topic. Immediately after composing, the videotape was replayed to the student, and he or she was questioned about all observed composing behaviors. The entire researcher/student dialogue was audiotaped and later transcribed. (These transcriptions will be referred to as protocols.)

Phase three involved various analyses of the protocols, of the behaviors recorded on videotape, and of the notes and essays produced by the students. More specifically, I and my assistants tallied evidence of cognitive, cognitive/behavioral, and cognitive/attitudinal functions in the protocols, measured prewriting, planning, and pausing time, counted words produced and deleted on the assignment materials, scratch paper, and essays, and, finally, had the essays evaluated by two independent readers. All the resultant data were both analyzed separately and consolidated into full case studies. Combining a quantitative and qualitative analysis of videotape, protocol, and written product provided a multidimensional portrait of strictured and facile composing in 10 university students. This multidimensional perspective allowed me to validate as well as qualify a cognitive orientation toward writer's block.

2

The Study: Questionnaire and Stimulated-Recall Investigation— Procedures and Results

Questionnaire: Rationale and Method

I'll begin with a rationale for using questionnaires to investigate a phenomenon as complex as the composing process. Questionnaires can provide a way to quickly collect data on and partially diagnose large numbers of students experiencing a major composing disruption like writer's block, but self-reports on the composing process might not always be accurate. Charles Cooper and Lee Odell,[1] for example, found that though experienced writers reported that sound did not influence their lexical choices, such influence could be demonstrated. It seems, however, that the key issue with composing-process self-reports would be the *availability of a particular composing act to personal observation*. A number of my pilot interviews suggested composing-process difficulties associated with blocking, two of the most prominent being editing prematurely and lacking interpretive and writing strategies for dealing with complex material. Both of these are characterized by salient behaviors (e.g., not writing further until one's first paragraph is perfect) or experiences (e.g., having a difficult time writing on issues with many interpretations). It seems likely that these sorts of behaviors and experiences are accessible to questionnaire inquiry; reporting on them does not necessarily involve exploration of covert mental processes or subtle influences (such as the sound of language) on those processes.

Rather, all that is involved is the individual's survey of a personal history of gross composing behaviors and experiences. These pilot interviews also suggested that certain attitudes about writing and evaluation are associated with some cases of writer's block. Attitude questionnaires are an accepted form of social science investigation and have been successfully applied to writing apprehension by Daly and Miller.

Questionnaire investigation of writer's block, therefore, can be legitimate, but, though legitimate, is limited in the following ways: To increase chances of collecting valid data, I had to exclude questions on complex and/or idiosyncratic composing acts and attitudes, some of which appeared in "Rigid Rules." This sacrifice of large amounts of diverse, complicated data for more limited but more exact data is a recognized conundrum in measurement: the Bandwidth-Fidelity Dilemma.[2] The questionnaire is also limited by its cognitive orientation. This orientation yields data to confirm, alter, or reject the conceptualization that informs the present study, but the focus excludes potential data on psychodynamic, motivational, and situational influences on writer's block. Again, a variation of the Bandwidth-Fidelity Dilemma. These considerations in mind, I began developing the questionnaire.

Early questionnaire items grew out of pilot interviews and were deleted or refined through subsequent administrations of the questionnaire (a total of four preliminary administrations with 184, 114, 38, and 64 students respectively). A fifth administration involved 351 undergraduates representing a broad range of majors, SAT scores, and writing experience. It was from this administration that I selected the students who will be the focus of the upcoming stimulated-recall investigation. Though this fifth version of the questionnaire was sound, I saw that a few items could be further refined. Therefore, I constructed a sixth version and administered it to 294 undergraduates who also represented a broad range of majors, SAT scores, and writing experience. This final version was composed of 24 items which, as with the penultimate version, could be subsumed under five subscales. Each item included an "Almost Always" to "Almost Never" Likert-type response sequence. The subscales and two items from each follow:

Blocking (this subscale provides a set of behavioral indicators of writer's block). "There are times when I sit at my desk for hours, unable to write a thing." "While writing a paper, I'll hit places that keep me stuck for an hour or more." *Lateness* (i.e., missing deadlines. A behavioral subscale, not as consistent an indicator of writer's block as Blocking). "I have to hand in assignments late because I can't get the words down on paper." "I run over deadlines because I get stuck while trying to write my papers." *Premature Editing* (i.e., editing too early in the composing process. A cognitive/behavioral subscale). "I'll wait until I've found just the right phrase." "Each sentence I write has to be just right before I'll go on to the next sentence." *Strategies for Complexity* (i.e., not possessing adequate strategies for interpreting and writing on complex material. A cognitive/behavioral subscale). "There are times when I'm not sure how to organize all the information I've gathered for a paper." "I have trouble figuring out how to write on issues that have many interpretations." *Attitudes* (i.e., feelings and beliefs about writing and evaluation. A cognitive/attitudinal subscale). "I think my writing is good." "My teachers are familiar with so much good writing that my writing must look bad by comparison."

The entire questionnaire is presented in Appendix A.

Questionnaire: Results

In order to refine the instrument, I and my assistants performed a number of statistical analyses on each version of the questionnaire. Presenting and exploring the results of these analyses inevitably involves one in a great deal of detail and a highly specialized statistical terminology. For present purposes, I will sidestep such an elaborate presentation and offer instead a summary of the results of the final (that is, the sixth) questionnaire's administration. (Tabular presentations of the results are in app. B.) A full discussion of the analyses of the fourth and fifth questionnaires can be found in "The Cognitive Dimension of Writer's Block: An Examination of University Students."[3]

A very important concern when analyzing questionnaire results is the consistency of individuals' responses. One measure of consistency derives from the fact that questionnaire items within a given subscale are designed to be relatively similar; thus, ideally, an individual's responses to these items should be relatively similar. So, for example, if a student checks "Almost Always" on "I'll wait until I've found just the right phrase," she is hopefully responding similarly ("Almost Always," "Often") to other Premature Editing items rather than responding in scattered fashion. Now, how does one determine the degree to which *all* students taking the questionnaire at any one time are responding consistently? An answer is provided by a statistical procedure called reliability analysis which provides a measure of the average consistency of response within a subscale. Consistency of response is represented by a coefficient that ranges from .0 to 1.0. Reliability coefficients for the sixth run of the writer's block questionnaire ranged from .72 to .87 with a respectable median coefficient of .84.

Responses can be consistent within subscales, but the subscales themselves might not be conceptually valid. They may be unrelated to each other where some relation is conceptually expected or, conversely, may overlap so dramatically that they might well be measuring similar rather than relatively distinct phenomena. This study's preliminary model holds that the subscales Lateness, Premature Editing, Strategies for Complexity, and Attitudes are all related to Blocking (the main behavioral indicator of writer's block) but measure different aspects of it. Therefore, a pattern of moderate correlations should emerge among Blocking and other subscales. This pattern resulted. Correlations between Blocking and each of the remaining subscales ranged from .37 to .59 with a median correlation of 40.5.

Reliability of items within subscales and correlations of subscales with each other can be significant, but fundamental questions about the legitimacy of the questionnaire would still remain. For example, something that researchers and teachers would certainly want is a measure of how well the cognitive/behavioral and cognitive/attitudinal subscales account for the behaviors pinpointed in the Blocking subscale. The cognitive orientation that informs the entire study posits a relationship between these cognitive subscales and Blocking. Do questionnaire responses confirm that relationship? A procedure called regression analysis provides an answer by enabling one to predict scores on the Blocking subscale from scores on the other subscales. A regression analysis demonstrated that the subscale scores predicted the Blocking score quite well (52 percent of the variance on the Blocking subscale scores was accounted for by the scores on the other subscales). Put in terms of this study's definition and model of writer's block, the behavior of missing deadlines, the cognitive/behavioral difficulties of editing prematurely and lacking strategies for complex writing assignments, and the cognitive/attitudinal problems associated with evaluation—as measured by the questionnaire items—provided a good prediction of the Blocking responses. Considering that the Blocking items do not present an exhaustive description of all manifestations of writer's block and considering, as well, the numerous cognitive variables (e.g., various rigid rules and misleading assumptions) that are too idiosyncratic to be measured by the questionnaire, accounting for 52 percent of the variance provides confirmation of the study's assumption that a considerable dimension of writer's block involves cognitive/behavioral and cognitive/attitudinal variables.

Stimulated Recall: Rationale and Method

To date, composing-process researchers have relied, for the most part, on one of two investigative methods: post-hoc interviews[4] and speaking-aloud protocol analysis.[5] In conducting post-hoc interviews, the researcher, having closely observed a writer composing, questions the writer about his just-completed writing behaviors. In conducting speaking-aloud protocol investigations, the researcher instructs a writer to verbalize everything passing through her mind as she writes. The writer's flow of speech is tape-recorded and later analyzed.

Ann Matsuhashi[6] has attempted a third method, a form of stimulated recall. Rather than simply relying on a student's memory during post-hoc interviews, Matsuhashi used the student's just-completed essay to prod recall of composing processes, using her detailed notes to direct her questions.

When I began my own investigations, I was not aware of Matsuhashi's work, but if I had been it would have supported my hunch that stimulated recall would be the most appropriate means with which to study writer's block. Though a major advantage of post-hoc interviews is that they are unobtrusive, they rely too heavily on memory and might not reveal the complexities of process hinted at by my pilot studies. As for speaking-aloud protocol analysis, it does not always work; some writers cannot talk aloud while they write.[7] Also, it is possible that some writers would focus on processes that could be easily and sensibly reported,[8] thus, again, leading one away from the possible complexities of stymied composing. And, of course, a major concern is the obtrusiveness of speaking-aloud procedures. Speaking aloud while writing could further tie up an already stymied process or, conversely, focus a writer's attention on the writing task, thus forestalling what William Styron has called the "one long, fantastic daydream"[9] that can characterize some writers' barrier to the page. Thus it was that I chose an alternative technique as the investigative method for this study.

Stimulated recall is a decision-making, problem-solving research procedure pioneered by Benjamin Bloom. During the procedure, an event is audiotaped and then played back to the participant(s) *soon after* the completion of the event. The key assumption is that the replay will stimulate recall of mental processes occurring during the event in question. Though the participant is encouraged to speak freely and stop the tape at will to elaborate on specific behaviors, the experimenter must be continually alert during replay— asking questions, stopping the tape, probing. Bloom, who has tested the validity and reliability of this procedure, believes that "a subject may be enabled to relive an original situation with great vividness and accuracy."[10] Furthermore, "this type of investigation can be carried on in such a way as to have only minimal effect on the nature of the original situation."[11] Nine years after Bloom's work, three researchers of interaction in psychotherapy added videotape to audiotape technology, thus unknowingly opening the door for composing-process research.[12]

Stimulated recall could be applied to composing research in the following way: a writer's page would be videotaped and immediately replayed; the writer would comment on his actions as the researcher questioned and prodded. Either writer or researcher could stop the tape. The dialogue would be audiotaped, transcribed, and analyzed.

But stimulated recall has its limitations: (1) Though not as obtrusive as speaking-aloud techniques, it does introduce the unnatural (e.g., cameras, prescribed positioning of paper) into the writing situation. Post-hoc interviews, of course, do not intrude at all.

(2) Stimulated recall does not provide an immediate rendering of mental activity; those activities are triggered into recall, not verbalized as they occur. (3) A stimulated-recall protocol can lack the precision found in speaking-aloud protocols. For example, during a two-minute pause, a writer might daydream for 20 seconds, mentally rehearse a sentence for 40 seconds, daydream again for 30 seconds, and think of his audience for 30 seconds. During a stimulated-recall session, the writer could remember that he was daydreaming, rehearsing a sentence, and considering his audience, but he might not recall the order of these activities and certainly could not report precisely on the time spent on each activity. If, however, the writer were speaking aloud (and if speaking aloud did not forestall daydreaming), a researcher would have access to the order of mental activities and the exact time spent on each. (4) Finally, stimulated recall works best when a remnant of a particular mental activity is left on the page. Some activity—say strictly mental rehearsal of a sentence—leaves no remnant and thus might not be stimulated into recall. Speaking-aloud protocols would reveal such activities.

But these limitations are outweighed by the advantages. Though not as unobtrusive as post-hoc interviews, stimulated-recall procedures do not substantially interfere with composing. Furthermore, stimulated recall does not lead a student to simplify or to hold to the task and—major advantage—allows a researcher to probe (without interfering with the flow of written language) and thus uncover rules, assumptions, strategies, and conflicts that might otherwise go unvoiced.

Subjects for the Study

Subjects were drawn from the pool of 351 students who filled out the fifth version of the writer's block questionnaire. Ten subjects (and two pilot subjects) were chosen according to the following criteria: (1) extreme high or low scores on the Blocking subscale, (2) extreme scores on the cognitive process and attitude subscales, and (3) representative range of English experience, measured on a scale of 1 (lowest) to 8 (highest).[13] These criteria make it possible to explore, within a limited sample, how high-blockers differ from low-blockers when English experience and scores on selected process

Table 1

Students Selected for Stimulated-Recall Composing Study

Name	Gender*	Year	Major	VSAT†	GPA†	Eng. Exp.‡	Reasons for Selection
High-blockers							
Stephanie	F	Fr.	Undecl.	400	2.18	Category 3	High level of Blocking and Complexity problems
Terryl	M	Jr.	English	514	3.29	Category 7	High level of Blocking and Editing problems
Ruth	F	Sr.	English	580	3.50	Category 8	High level of Blocking and Editing problems
Gary	M	Sr.	Biochem.	600	3.90	Category 7	High level of Blocking, Editing, and Complexity problems
Debbie	F	Fr.	Undecl.	400	1.92	Category 1	High level of Blocking, Complexity, and Attitude problems
Liz	F	Sr.	English	610	2.67	Category 7	High level of Blocking and Lateness problems but moderate to low scores on Editing, Complexity, and Attitude
Low-blockers							
Glenn	M	So.	Theater Arts	600	3.85	Category 6	Low level of Blocking, Editing, and Complexity problems
Sandra	F	Fr.	Undecl.	520	3.39	Category 3	Low level of Blocking, Editing, and Complexity problems
Amy	F	Jr.	Biochem.	550	2.93	Category 5	Low level of Blocking, Editing, and Complexity problems
Dana	F	Fr.	Undecl.	450	3.45	Category 1	Low level of Blocking, Lateness, and Editing problems but high scores on Complexity and Attitude

Notes:

*There are at least two explanations for the inordinate number of females: (1) The sample contained twice as many females as males. (2) Two of the three students who couldn't participate were males; the two subsequent appropriate subjects were females. The original 10 subjects would have provided a better gender balance.

†The mean VSAT for UCLA freshmen (in 1979) was 486. The mean (1979) GPA of UCLA freshmen was 2.7, sophomores 2.8, juniors 2.9, seniors 3.0. A few students excepted, this was an academically successful group.

‡A reminder: 1 is low, 8 is high.

and attitude subscales are varied. I chose more high-blockers than low-blockers to assure multiple perspectives on stymied composing.

The 10 students are listed in Table 1. GPA's and verbal SAT scores were not included in the selection criteria; they were obtained from records after selection.

The Writing Environment: The Setting

Before going to the taping room, students met individually with me in my office. I compiled a writing history, discussed the study, and assured them of confidentiality. Fortunately none of the students seemed nervous or shy. After approximately one-half hour in my office, we went to a small classroom that was equipped as a studio.

A pad of paper was clipped to a desk; behind the desk—out of the student's sight but focused on the pad—was a videotape camera. Another camera was positioned across the room to catch the student from waist up. (The two cameras would produce one split-screen image via a special-effects generator.) No lights were necessary because half of one wall was a window. Viewing monitors were placed out of sight in an adjoining room. Each student was filmed individually and, once the cameras were running, was alone.

Before taping, I had students freewrite. I arranged the writing pad to suit each student's posture and accordingly adjusted the camera alongside the desk. Once a student was comfortable, I clipped the pad in place for filming and gave the assignment (which will be discussed shortly) along with the following instructions:

> Write this essay as you normally would. Do whatever you usually do when you sit down to compose a school paper. I ask only two things of you: (1) Line out rather than scratch out words you write but choose not to use. (2) Don't rip up any paper you've used. The video cassettes I'm using run for one hour, so after one hour, I'll return, and we'll watch the tape of your essay. If you don't finish, that's o.k. This is not a test.
>
> To make this a little more realistic, a little more like a school writing situation, I and one other English instructor will evaluate your and the other students' papers. If you don't finish, we'll evaluate you on what you've written.

The student was allowed to read the assignment materials, reflect on them (but not yet mark them) and ask me clarifying questions. When the student felt ready to write, I turned on the camera and left the room.

Two aspects of the instructions need further explanation:

Evaluation. In popular culture, fear of evaluation is touted as a major cause of writer's block. Evaluation is clearly part of the school environment, and evaluation plays into this study's hypotheses on blocking as well. Evaluation, therefore, had to be introduced into this obviously artificial setting. The danger for the validity of the study, of course, was that students would discount or devalue the proposed evaluation, realizing full well that the exercise did not count for much. All students, however, reported writing as they usually do, with the effort they usually expend. They all thought the topic challenging, and all seemed concerned with producing good writing and good ideas. (Sample comments from the protocols: "But I did want to write something that sounded halfway intelligent"; "Something like this—I want to write it.")

Time. The 60-minute limit is fairly common in composing-process research, one reason being that more generous boundaries would yield an unwieldy amount of data. But even if this were not the case, the present study would have required a potentially constricting time limit because it attempted to simulate some aspects of the school environment—time constraints and evaluative contexts. How did the student work within these restrictions? Did he or she heed my direction and ignore the time limit, or did the prospect of evaluation or simply the 60-minute boundary itself impede or spark production?

Though the presence of a (potentially perceived) deadline and evaluation make this study realistic, the camera, fixed note pad, and experimental context mark it as unusual. However, it will be recalled that students were given whatever time they needed to get used to the setting. Fortunately, no student needed more than about five minutes to settle in. And though half the students reported some awareness of the camera (e.g., "I felt like we were wasting film") or the experimental setting (e.g., "I thought about this being an experiment") during the first few minutes of taping, they soon got involved in the assignment and did not display or report further environmental distractions.

The Writing Environment: The Topic

Since the attempt here was to simulate the school writing environment, the substance and mode of the topic should represent university assignments. I decided that the mode of discourse would be exposition, more specifically, analysis—that is, exposition that requires that a body of data, an event, or a situation be examined from a particular theoretical perspective.[14] The substance of the assignment should reflect a typical introductory course issue, perhaps one from the social sciences or humanities, yet should not fall neatly into the realm of one but not another student's major. Furthermore, the assignment should be built on a reading passage, thus enabling all students to begin with a more or less equal knowledge base. This passage should present no significant "readability" or interpretation problems. The following assignment met these criteria: Students were given a three-page case history of Angelo Cacci, a 32-year-old man visiting a counseling center with complaints of depression. The fundamental narrative contains a good deal of information, is accessible and jargon-free. Students were to interpret Angelo's situation in light of a passage from Karl Jaspers' *Man in the Modern Age*. The passage, typical of alienation theory, roots the cause of contemporary malaise in meaningless work. (The entire assignment can be found in app. C.) I pretested the assignment with two remedial-level students, two juniors in life and physical sciences, and one senior English major. None had problems reading, understanding, or responding to the materials.

Perhaps the major weakness of the present study was that the student was limited to a single topic. If a particular student was hampered by the topic, then his or her writing performance was negatively affected. Still, because of the study's investigative methodology, I decided to proceed with a single topic. If I had given two or more topics, students would either have had to wait until all were completed before viewing the tapes (thus extending the time between composing and recalling) or write on one topic after writing and recalling another (thus contaminating the composing of any but the first essay). Either possibility would be undesirable.

It could be argued, however, that, given the purpose of the study, a single topic was appropriate. The attempt here was not to elicit a student's best performance but to observe him or her responding to a typical situation. School-based assignments do not always offer choice of topic. How would the student work within such constraints? More to the point, would high-blockers and low-blockers differ in the way they set out to interpret materials and respond to assignments that they did not choose?

Artifacts of the study (camera, fixed pad) aside, there could be fundamental objection to the nature of the writing environment itself: precisely because it copied the school setting, it may have contributed to, and even caused, many of the problems that mar student prose. Sharon Crowley, taking the lead from Richard Lloyd-Jones' statement that "excessive pressure [on writers] produces conventional responses," impugns the "academic context in which students' writing is done, with its attendant machinery of grades, assignments, due dates, and other pressures which produce 'conventional responses.'"[15] No argument. But since this was a study of writer's block in undergraduates, the constricting reality of the undergraduate writing environment had to be copied. How high-blockers and low-blockers would function within that environment was part of what I wanted to explore.

Conducting Stimulated Recall

The student and I sat side by side at a table, a viewing monitor in front of us, both a videotape and audiotape recorder before us. The image on the monitor was split; three-quarters of the screen showed the student's page; one-quarter, the student from waist up.

Before we viewed the tape, I asked the student three questions: (1) Was this representative of the way you compose? (2) Do you think the way you compose is similar to the way your peers compose? (3) Do you think the way you compose is similar to the way professional writers compose? I then explained how stimulated recall works:

> As we watch the tape I'll be asking you questions about what you were doing. At times I'll even stop the videotape so we can examine a marginal note, a word choice, a revision and so forth. As you watch your writing

unfold, try to recall what you were thinking at the time; try to put your mind back into the task. Anytime you remember something, say it, interrupt me, stop the tape if you want.

I'm interested in finding out what you were thinking when you were writing, and it doesn't matter at all to me if those thoughts were silly or profound.

I'll audio-record our conversation so I don't have to divide my attention by taking notes.[16]

As indicated in the above explanation, I constantly questioned all writing behaviors but was especially interested in notes and marginalia, lexical to thesis-level deletions and additions, and pausing. I also stopped the tape at random points during the smooth flow of prose. Finally, I questioned suggestive facial expressions—from quizzical frowns to blank stares. The student was also able to stop the tape and comment. The entire dialogue was audiotaped; the tape was later transcribed, the resultant transcript (protocol) providing data for quantitative and case-study analyses.

Analyzing Stimulated-Recall Protocols

At first glance, a protocol from a stimulated-recall session looks like drama dialogue. But the researcher's statements are all of a kind: restatements of what the student says, descriptions of the writing behavior being replayed on the video monitor, and simple inquiries. These statements and questions serve both to focus the student's attention and to make the resultant protocol understandable in the absence of the video image. The researcher's questions and statements, then, are solely a device; it is, therefore, the student's responses that become the subject of analysis.

I analyzed this study's protocols via several methods. In the present chapter I will offer a tally of cognitive functions and composing behaviors displayed in the protocols (the tally being informed by the conceptualization of writer's block presented in chap. 1). I will also offer measurements of prewriting, planning, and pausing time, tabulations of words produced and deleted, and evaluations of the students' essays. In the next chapter, I will flesh out the aforementioned data with two case studies. But before proceeding, a digression is in order. Because there is some controversy about the legitimacy of self-report data,[17] I will present, in some detail, a rationale for and description of the procedures I used to analyze the stimulated-recall protocols.

Though stimulated recall is a validated procedure and though I conducted the interviews with some care, a stimulated-recall protocol can contain some reports that are not accurate. K. Anders Ericsson and Herbert Simon[18] distinguish between mental processes that a subject attends to and reports on directly vs. mental processes that are not directly accessed and thus are speculated on by the subject. Unfortunately for present purposes, Ericsson and Simon concentrate on speaking-aloud procedures and do not treat stimulated-recall techniques in their discussion. Still, their distinction can be applied to stimulated-recall data: the researcher must note when a subject is reporting directly on immediate behaviors (and, as Benjamin Bloom has demonstrated, attendant mental processes) as they pass before him on the video monitor, and when the subject is drifting into reflection and speculation on present or past composing behaviors and situations. To protect against an intrusion of possibly inaccurate hypothesizing and inferring, I based my analysis on student reports that originated from behaviors viewed on the monitor and corroborated by events on the screen, features of the student's essay, or reports voiced in other sections of the protocol. For example, if a student said, "I am trying to decide between 'affect' and 'effect'" or "You shouldn't use 'affect' to describe a major change in something," and the monitor showed him pausing and/or his essay showed "af . . ." scratched out and "effect" in place, then his report was judged accurated. If the monitor showed the student writing smoothly along and if his essay showed no trace of a decision about word choice, then the report was not considered valid. (This demand for corroborating evidence might be overly stringent, for, in the case of the above example, a writer certainly could make decisions about diction in a split second while writing and not pause at all. But since no theory-based validating criteria have been established for stimulated-recall data, I prefer to treat such data conservatively.) Fortunately, most reports stemming from behaviors viewed on the monitor were supported by other data.

I conducted the analysis of the protocols in the following way. I first examined the protocols myself, labeling the behaviors and implied processes with my cognitive taxonomy. I later excerpted sections of the protocols, in necessary cases providing a few sentences of context, and had these analyzed by a second rater who had been trained to use the taxonomy. (Reliability was determined by percent of inter-rater agreement, which was .94.)[19] Following is a section of protocol complete with description of context:

> This comes from Liz's first 10 minutes of composing. She has just reread the quotation from Karl Jaspers and is jotting interpretive notes on the assignment sheet, underneath the quotation. She writes "is saying that not having creative, generative work is," stops, and begins changing her words. As soon as she sees herself beginning the sentence she says: "I didn't finish it because I lost the thought." She then begins commenting on her sentence production.
>
> *Liz*: . . . I'm starting a sentence. I'm saying, "That sounds bad."
> *Researcher*: You're writing a sentence.
> *Liz*: And I stopped it.
> *Researcher*: O.K. On the instruction sheet here you write . . . "is saying that not having creative, generative work is the . . ." And then you stop. (After pausing, Liz scratches out "is the" and replaces it with "causes.")
> *Liz*: You're not supposed to have passive verbs.
> *Researcher*: So you scratch that out and put "causes." (Liz then scratches out "is saying" and replaces it with "says.") Then you change another verb—"is saying" to "says."
> *Liz*: Which then turns out to be too colloquial. (A further long pause.)

According to my classificatory system, the entire passage represents premature editing. Liz's labeling of her sentence ("That sounds bad") is a negative evaluation. Her injunction ("You're not supposed to have passive verbs") is a rigid rule. (In the above context, it is also misapplied.) And the alteration of "is saying" to "says" combined with the tagging of that change as being "too colloquial" is classified as an instance of conflict. Occurrences of these and all other events, behaviors, and processes were tallied in each protocol.

Stimulated Recall: Results

A Tally of Cognitive Functions and Composing Behaviors

When protocol commentaries are categorized and tallied, rules, strategies, assumptions, etc., are reduced to equal weight. Thus, the occurrence but not the strength of a particular cognitive function in a particular student's composing process is recorded. Case studies in the next chapter will provide a sense of the idiosyncratic strengths of functions that are only tallied in protocol analysis.

Let me offer a rationale for the criteria I used in tallying cognitive functions and composing behaviors. Rules, assumptions, strategies, conflicts, and evaluations are mental occurrences. They could be affecting composing behaviors at a number of junctures, but that number cannot always be determined. So a specific rule, assumption, etc., will be counted only once, even if it is voiced at several points in the protocol. Premature editing, on the other hand, is an observable behavior, and each time it occurs (or is specifically circumvented), it affects the flow of prose. Thus, a tally of all occurrences (and circumventions) of premature editing will be useful. Some cognitive functions and composing behaviors (e.g., the rules "If a sentence sounds good, then it is good writing"; "Separate two clauses with a semicolon") could not be judged functional or nonfunctional in the context of the protocol. These were not tallied. Also, rules, assumptions, strategies, etc., that I conjectured but that were not explicitly stated by the student were not counted. A few conjectures will be presented—and will be labeled as conjecture—in the case studies. Again, I'm trying to assure the legitimacy of the results by treating data somewhat conservatively.

The numbers of high-blockers (six) and low-blockers (four) are not equal; therefore, it would make little sense to simply add up each group's responses. Instead, in Table 2 I'll present mean (average) numbers of cognitive functions and composing behaviors, high-blockers by low-blockers. Since the number of subjects is so small, traditional tests of statistical significance are inappropriate; differences between subjects would have to be massive to assure one that effects are not due to chance. Therefore, I'll discuss trends and differences in the means, but it must be kept in mind that the discussion is not confirmed statistically.

Comparing high-blockers and low-blockers on the 19 measures listed in Table 2, 13 of the measures go in a direction that supports this study's cognitive model. Three (Nonfunctional Denial or Modification of Rules, a lack of Interpretive Strategies for Complexity, and Positive Imagined Evaluation by Others) yield no difference (no instance of any of the categories was found). And three yield dif-

Table 2
Mean Number of Cognitive Functions and Composing Behaviors

	High-blockers	Low-blockers
Rules		
functional	.17	3.00
nonfunctional	1.17	.25
Denial or Modification of Rules		
functional	0	.50
nonfunctional	0	0
Misleading Assumptions	.83	0
Premature Editing	2.17	1.00
Premature Editing Circumvented	.83	2.75
Strategies for Complexity		
Interpretive Strategies		
functional	1.00	1.25
nonfunctional	.66	0
none	0	0
Writing Strategies		
functional	.83	2.00
nonfunctional	.17	.25
none	1.83	.75
Conflicting Rules, Assumptions, etc.	2.00	.25
Self-Evaluation		
negative	2.83	2.00
positive	.83	.75
Imagined Evaluation by Others		
negative	.17	.50
positive	0	0
discounts evaluation by others	.33	.50

ferences that run counter to the model, but the differences are quite small. Of the 13 remaining measures, the differences between the two groups on Rules, Misleading Assumptions, Premature Editing, Writing Strategies, and Conflict are most striking.

Compared to high-blockers, low-blockers expressed 17 times as many functional rules and only one-quarter the nonfunctional rules. Four of the six high-blockers voiced a misleading assumption, while none was expressed by a low-blocker. Low-blockers circumvented premature editing three times as often as high-blockers and enacted it half as frequently. Low-blockers wrote with the aid of over twice as many functional strategies as high-blockers and came up wanting approximately half as often. Finally, high-blockers were conflicted eight times more frequently than low-blockers.

The two groups did not register major differences on Interpretive Strategies or Evaluation. Most of the 10 students achieved an adequate to rich understanding of Jaspers and the case history. The strategic differences between high-blocker and low-blocker came at the writing stage. (Though most all students had trouble framing analytic expository discourse.) The closeness of the evaluation measures is interesting. It's a commonly held belief that blocking is very much related to being overly critical, perfectionistic, down on one's writing, etc. But these characteristics, insofar as they would emerge in specific evaluative comments, were not necessarily related to high-blockers or low-blockers in the admittedly small sample of 10.

With the above differences between the two groups in mind, it would be instructive to examine the students' composing behaviors and written products more closely. In stimulated-recall procedures, videotapes serve as a stimulus; they are valuable only as memory prods. But the tapes themselves could be used as records of process; easily quantifiable behaviors and characteristics could be tallied.

Time Allotted to Prewriting and Planning

Some high-blockers complain that it takes them a long time to get started—the initial thought, the first sentence. Table 3 offers several measures of the time this study's 10 students spent before they began formal drafting. Column 1 presents a measure of time spent simply rereading the assignment materials before writing of any kind began. Column 2 lists time spent writing on assignment sheets, case histories, and scratch paper.

For the sake of convenience, I will label the first column "prewriting" and the second "planning," though reading and thinking about a topic and structuring the results of that activity are not neatly separable acts. Therefore, in column 3 I will combine data from columns 1 and 2. The reader can choose either of the separate measures or the combined measure. I will work with all three.

The range of prewriting and planning measurements is so broad

Table 3
Time Spent Prewriting and Planning

	Column 1 Time elapsed from start of tape to first writing (Prewriting)	Column 2 Time spent glossing, scratch-writing (Planning)	Column 3 Columns 1 and 2 combined (Prewriting and Planning)
High-blockers			
Stephanie	8 min. 44 sec.	0	8:44
Terryl	5:46	1:26	7:12
Ruth	3:18	7:10	10:28
Gary	:56	45:34	46:30
Debbie	2:35	0	2:35
Liz	2:37	31:13	33:50
Low-blockers			
Glenn	11:33	0	11:33
Sandra	12:38	0	12:38
Amy	1:46	7:36	9:22
Dana	4:02	2:48	6:50

that calculations of average times would be misleading. It is more appropriate, then, to look at separate cases. Individual prewriting and planning styles are evident. Stephanie, Glenn, and Sandra spent a good deal of time rereading and contemplating the assignment but no time on lists, outlines, or sketches. Debbie, though in a more attenuated fashion, did the same. Conversely, Amy, and to an extreme degree, Gary, spent very little time thinking and rereading without the aid of pen and paper. Regardless of individual style, though, prewriting, particularly since Gordon Rohman's major work,[20] has been recognized as an essential dimension of the composing process. And the work of Linda Flower and John Hayes[21] has suggested that one mark of a good student writer is involvement in planning. However, combined prewriting and planning times (column 3) for two high-blockers, Gary and Liz, suggest that there is a point past which prewriting and planning might be dysfunctional. The student becomes more and more involved in a vortex of analyzing and plotting rather than in the development of discourse.

Pausing: Rescanning, Proofreading, and Reflecting

Let me begin by defining terms: Rescanning was classified as a clearly detectable rereading—a student's eyes moving to previous sentences, a student flipping back to other pages. Proofreading was time spent reading (presumably for correctness) once the essay was finished. Other cessations of writing would simply be labeled "regular pauses" or reflections—moments, the stimulated-recall protocols revealed, that were usually filled with idea-generating, word to sentence rehearsal, and reverie. I should emphasize that all three measures are of time elapsed when pen was *not* on paper. All are pauses of some type.

We exhort our students to think before writing. Table 4 displays the remarkable amount of time actually spent in thought: an average of one-half to two-thirds of these students' time was spent pausing, not forming words on paper. If we compare the two subsamples, we see that the average length of total high-blockers' pauses is not much longer than that of low-blockers (23.1 seconds vs. 22.5 seconds). The difference comes in average number of total pauses (105 vs. 83.3). The end-result is that for this 60-minute essay, high-blockers, on the average, paused 9.1 minutes longer than low-blockers. Two of the subcategories reflect these differences—high-blockers spent more time in regular pauses and rescanning pauses (though the range of average length of rescanning pauses is so broad that the mean is misleading). Since only one high-blocker (Debbie) finished her essay and since she did not proofread, no formal proofreading time was logged for that group. All low-blockers finished their essays, though Glenn chose not to proofread (or perhaps did so inconspicuously while composing).

Sharon Pianko has proposed that "the act of reflection during composing . . . behaviorally manifested as pauses and rescanning" is a highly significant aspect of the composing process.[22] (She did not separately consider proofreading.) While there is little doubt that Pianko is right in championing reflection, the above data suggest that, as with prewriting and planning, there is a highly individual point past which pausing can be detrimental. Sondra Perl, for example, found that her remedial students—vigilantly searching for error—paused so frequently that the flow of their ideas was disrupted.[23] Whether one is scrutinizing or rehearsing or daydreaming, the clock still ticks and the word is potentially held back from

Table 4
Number and Mean Length of Regular Pauses, Rescanning Pauses, and Proofreading Pauses

	Regular Pauses		Rescanning Pauses		Proofreading Pauses		Total Pauses	
	Number	Average Length (in Seconds)	Number	Average Length	Number	Average Length	Number	Average Length
High-blockers								
Stephanie	75	20.5	5	55.8	0	0	80	24.5
Terryl	67	36.6	2	118.0	0	0	69	35.4
Ruth	154	15.7	0	0	0	0	154	15.7
Gary	156	15.6	4	78.2	0	0	160	17.6
Debbie	81	19.5	4	124.5	0	0	85	24.9
Liz	62	28.9	20	52.6	0	0	82	34.4
Mean:	99.2		5.8		0		105	
Weighted Mean:		20.5		68.0		0		23.1
			Average Time Spent Pausing: 40.5 Minutes					
Low-blockers								
Glenn	69	14.5	3	46.3	0	0	72	15.8
Sandra	62	25.8	0	0	12	42.5	74	28.2
Amy	53	17.3	7	47.9	19	40.0	79	26.5
Dana	106	16.6	1	384.0	1	27.0	108	20.0
Mean:	72.5		2.8		8		83.3	
Weighted Mean:		18.2		78.0		40.5		22.5
			Average Time Spent Pausing: 31.4 Minutes					

paper. Liz and Gary, two high-blockers, produced essays of less than one paragraph.

Tabulation of Words Produced

Word counts are as reductionistic as measures of elapsed time. But a tabulation of words marked, produced, and deleted could provide, from assignment material and essay, a crude process chart—a further perspective on how time is allotted. In Table 5, columns 1 and 2 list words marked or written on the assignment materials. These give some hint (though certainly not an exclusive one) of care and style of rereading of and reflection on the assignment itself. If the student moved to scratch paper or used the instruction sheet as scratch paper, then words written there are tallied in column 4. First draft words are listed in column 6. Deletions in each of the three categories are presented in columns 3, 5, and 7. And since it is possible to consider all writing—from annotation to draft—as an evolving text, total words produced and deleted are presented in columns 8 and 9. The following criteria were used in the tabulation: Writing on the assignment sheet or case history that clarifies or connects issues in these texts is considered explication. Writing on the bottom or back of the assignment sheet or on separate paper that lists ideas or strings phrases together or frames an outline is considered "scratch." Writing that is clearly an attempt to frame an essay is considered a draft.

The range of tabulations in columns 1–5 is so broad that means are misleading. Means are more appropriate in columns 6–9, though they still should be read with caution. Therefore, individual cases as well as means, when fitting, will be discussed below.

Again, individual composing styles are evident. Glenn and Stephanie reread and planned with pen suspended and then moved straight to the production of their texts. Ruth and Amy underlined and glossed the assignment materials a good deal before they began drafting. Both these styles suggest that some degree of mental planning of the draft can go on when one is rereading or explicating assignments. Formal or "scratch" outlines or sketches or lists do not have to be produced for planning to occur. Liz followed a more "prescribed" sequence, working with assignment materials as well as scratch paper before producing her draft. But, from word counts as well as the elapsed time perspective, an overemphasis on pre-

Table 5

Tabulation of Words Marked on Materials and Words Produced and Deleted on Scratch Paper and Drafts

Column	1 Words Marked on Materials	2 Words Written on Materials	3 Words Deleted on Materials	4 Words Produced on Scratch Paper	5 Words Deleted on Scratch Paper	6 Words Produced on Draft	7 Words Deleted on Draft	8 Total Words Written	9 Total Words Deleted
High-blockers									
Stephanie	0	0	0	0	0	334	37	334	37
Terryl	19	5	0	0	0	263	4	268	4
Ruth	117	61	0	0	0	608	30	669	30
Gary	142	353	44	0	0	59	37	402	81
Debbie	0	2	0	0	0	320	11	322	11
Liz	67	128	5	129	20	45	4	302	29
Mean	57.5	91.5	8.2	21.5	3.3	271.5	20.5	383	32
Range	0–142	0–353	0–99	0–129	0–20	45–608	4–37	268–669	4–81
Low-blockers									
Glenn	0	0	0	0	0	572	39	572	39
Sandra	31	2	0	0	0	330	29	332	29
Amy	57	63	0	0	0	355	55	418	55
Dana	0	0	0	31	0	369	1	400	1
Mean	22.0	16.3	0	7.8	0	406.5	31	430.5	31
Range	0–57	0–63	0–0	0–31	0–0	330–572	1–55	332–572	1–55

writing and planning is evident in the productions of Liz and particularly Gary. Eighty-five percent of both Liz's and Gary's total words never appeared on their drafts, and Gary's draft, when one considers that 39 percent of its words were edited out as he wrote, was still very much a developing text.

Editing styles are also evident. Terryl, Debbie, and Dana either settled for the first word that came to mind or made a number of lexical choices in their heads rather than trying out options on paper. The other students worked out some of their options on paper. For that fact, Gary seemed to be continually sorting through options, even when simply glossing his assignment materials.

Columns 6 and 8 give a simple measure of fluency. On the average (and Gary and Liz skew that average), high-blockers produced 135 fewer words on drafts than their low-blocking peers. But if one considers all writing as unfolding text, that disparity is considerably reduced. Both groups produced close to the same number of words. The high-blockers in this study were not sitting before the proverbial blank page; their pages of materials or scratch paper or drafts were filled with words. Where the words fell is another story. As was seen in the previous analysis of elapsed time, the issue here is efficiency. Gary and Liz produced but produced disproportionately, and Terryl produced a relatively brief text. But what about the other three? For that fact, Ruth generated more words than anybody. Case studies in my dissertation[24] reveal the cause behind this somewhat surprising fluency. While I had feared that the 60-minute deadline might further stymie blocked writers, it turned out that the time limit served as a goad to some high-blockers, causing them to either override their usually restricting editing rules and produce acceptable prose, or get anxious and produce lengthy but incoherent prose. I will return to the issue of deadlines in the Afterword.

Measures of time and word counts have been helpful in highlighting certain aspects of writer's block, but this tallying would mean little if the work produced by the two groups proved to be of equal merit. It is time to consider the foregoing in light of reader response to the essays the students submitted.

Evaluation of the Essays

The essays were evaluated with a revised version of the UCLA Freshman Summer Program analytic scale (see app. D). Readers

Table 6
Analytic Scale Evaluations of Student Essays

		Total Score (Range: 0–39)
High-blockers		
Stephanie		20.50
Terryl		24.75
Ruth		17.00
Gary		10.75
Debbie		20.00
Liz		12.50
	Mean	17.60
Low-blockers		
Glenn		23.75
Sandra		19.25
Amy		27.50
Dana		21.25
	Mean	22.90

also wrote summary comments. Each analytic category ranges, in increments of .5, from 0 to 3. The maximum score is 39. The categories and their weights follow:

Punctuation and Spelling: multiply by 1
Grammar: × 1
Thesis and Evidence: × 2
Organization and Development: × 2
Sentence Style: × 2
Diction: × 2
Quality of Analysis: × 3

Punctuation, spelling, and grammar errors are given least weight here because some such errors could be the results of inadequate proofreading time. The quality of the writer's analysis is given most weight to assure reward for insightful expression.

The essays were evaluated separately by two Teaching Assistants who had each taught composition for four years. They also had a good deal of experience using the scale. They were not told about the study or about the backgrounds and writing behaviors of the students. All they knew was the assignment and the fact that the essays were composed in 60 minutes. I stressed the 60-minute deadline and explained that they should read these as in-class and not prepared papers, and, therefore, as much as possible, should evaluate students on the merit of what they produced, however little that may be. Reliability was determined by percent of inter-rater agreement, which was 93.[25] The scores reported in Table 6 are the averages of both readers' independent evaluations.[26]

Given most of the students' GPA's and experience, the scores are fairly low. Most likely the time boundary and topic complexity limited the possibility of receiving a score above Amy's 27.5. It seems, though, that whatever the variables, they worked more against high-blockers than low-blockers: there is a 5.3 point difference between the means of the two groups. Even with the low scores of Gary and Liz deleted, the means still reflect a 2.34 point difference. (I should add that my recommendation to consider the merit of incomplete work apparently restricted the range of scores. Liz and Gary's essays would most likely receive even lower evaluations in other grading situations.)

Though measures of time spent prewriting, planning, and pausing, and tallies of words a writer submits are simplistic criteria for judging merit, it is clear that exceptionally limited production negatively affects audience response. Two of the high-blockers, Liz and Gary, received the readers' lowest evaluations.

3

Case Studies of Two Students

OF THE 10 STUDENTS CHOSEN FOR THE STIMULATED-RECALL study, six were designated as high-blockers by the questionnaire and four were designated as low-blockers. Though the tallies of cognitive functions, composing behaviors, and essay features and the reader evaluations of the essays all suggest differences between these two groups, some students more neatly fit the study's conceptualization and hypotheses than others. The high-blockers Liz and Gary and the low-blockers Glenn and Amy most dramatically illustrated blocked vs. fluid composing and confirmed the study's cognitive orientation. Three other high-blockers (Terryl, Debbie, and Stephanie) were, surprisingly enough, impelled by the study's deadline and wrote more than they reported they usually would under less restricting circumstances. Still, their protocols illustrate the kinds of problems that are related to their blocking. Finally, one high-blocker (Ruth) became anxious and frantically wrote a good deal of disconnected, erratic prose. Of the six high-blockers, only one (Stephanie) presented problems for which the study's cognitive model had markedly limited explanatory power. Her composing problems were more related to self-image and self-reliance than to cognitive interferences like rigid rules.

I present two of the 10 case studies found in "The Cognitive Dimension of Writer's Block"; these two cases provide a vivid illustration of the study's thesis.

A word on the variety of citations presented in the case studies. Most will be student reports from the protocols, though responses to the questionnaire (e.g., "Always," "Occasionally"), my questions, passages from the essays, and readers' comments will also be presented. *Unless otherwise noted in the text, all citations will be student protocol commentary.*

One last note: Each case study is preceded by a typed verbatim copy of the student's essay. Nothing is corrected, but words the student lined out are not included.

A High-blocker: Liz

Liz is a senior English major with a 610 VSAT and a 2.67 GPA. Her writing experience placed her in category 7 (1 is lowest, 8 highest). She received a score of 12.50 (on a scale of 1–39) on her essay. Her questionnaire results follow: 1.9 standard deviations[1] above the Blocking mean (i.e., in the direction of blocking); 1.4 standard deviations above the Lateness mean; .6 of a standard deviation above the Premature Editing mean; .05 of a standard deviation above the Strategies for Complexity mean; .1 of a standard deviation above the Attitude mean.

Liz's Essay

The depression Angelo experiences and the dis-continuity Jaspers describes can both be accounted for, at least in some sense by the quality of city life; by the modern experience. Angelo's "blues" for example may result directly from breakup with his girlfriend but even if they do

Liz's Session

Overview. At the 60-minute deadline, Liz turned in a draft of 45 words—a topic sentence and part of a second, apparently qualifying, sentence. This extremely brief product, however, belied the amount of writing she actually produced. After rereading the assignment materials for 2½ minutes, Liz began underlining the Jaspers passage and the case history, glossing the former and jotting down fragments and sentences on scratch paper. Liz did not pause a great number of times while writing (62), but her pauses were relatively long (28.9 seconds on the average). During most of these pauses, Liz was weighing ideas and rehearsing sentences. She often spoke

aloud and gestured with her hand while rehearsing, apparently testing the rhythm of her sentences, measuring rhythm with the waves
of her hand in the air.

From the beginning, Liz "was trying to make a connection . . .
between" the passages. (A sentence from the first page of her scratch
paper revealed this attempt at fusion: "Jaspers attributes the personal unhappiness of people like Cacci to the noncreative nature of
their jobs.") But, at the same time, Liz was wrestling with the legitimacy of the Jaspers passage itself, raising a solid argument against
the romanticism inherent in the work of mass society critics: "I've
heard this type of argument before, and they say, 'Farmers, oh, they
grow. They have such a wonderful life.' And it's not true. They can
be real, real, you know, just as unhappy and miserable and a lot
worse than we are." Simultaneous with her attempts to effect a connection between Angelo's life and Jaspers' vision (mentally arguing
with Jaspers' vision all the while), Liz was also making a number of
lexical to phrase-level changes in her glossing and rough draft.
Within the first 10 minutes of writing, Liz made the following alterations: passive constructions were changed to active ones; "to be"
forms were changed to more striking verbs; certain words (e.g.,
"says") were rejected as being "too colloquial"; other words (e.g.,
"like") were rejected for being "too simple . . . too easy"; clauses
were rejected or accepted by the way they sounded; clauses were
also rejected for containing a preposition; and, finally, spelling was
corrected. These emendations were supported with rules like:
"You're not supposed to have passive verbs"; "You can't start a sentence with 'says'"; "If you can singsong it, it's not good stylistically."
Sometimes Liz's decisions were based on rules and concepts she did
not fully understand: "When he's [a textbook author] talking about
'to be' verbs, I don't really even understand what he's saying."
Other times, her rules and resulting word choices would conflict.
When she changed "is saying" to "says," she noted that the new
verb "would . . . be too colloquial" and thus would not be acceptable. Further on she wrote "to the noncreative nature of their jobs"
and said it "is good [because it sounds good], and it's bad because of
the 'of.'" Finally, there were times when Liz's preoccupation with
editing resulted in her forgetting her thought. Very early in the
hour she wrote an interpretive note under the Jaspers passage: "is
saying that not having creative (generative) work is the"; she stopped

and changed "is saying" to "says" and "is the" to "causes." Then came a long pause. She couldn't remember the rest of her insight. "That happens a lot," she later observed.

Through the second third of her hour, Liz continued to pause, rehearse, and jot down ideas on scratch paper. The ideas of this period were expressed in strings of sentences as Liz's disagreement with Jaspers (and her attempt to work that disagreement into the assignment) was becoming more evident (e.g., "The breakup between Angelo and his girlfriend is probably the reason for his depression. Jaspers, if you accept the little that is given in this selection, might attribute the breakup to the kind of job that he is talking about"). As Liz continued to attempt new sentences and rephrase old ones, it became obvious that she was trying to form an approach to the assignment that would allow her to work with Jaspers' vision while taking issue with it. This approach would become the stuff of a topic sentence as well as a conclusion, and, for Liz, thinking of some sort of a conclusion fairly early is important: "A place to end up. I always have that." But mid-way through the hour, she had not yet found her approach. When asked if, at this point, she could have told what her paper was going to be about, she replied, "No. No way." She was experiencing "real confusion" as she continued to think of and set down one and two sentence "blocks of information," wrestling with Jaspers all the while. Then, at this mid-point, she suddenly put her scratch paper aside and began the draft she would turn in, framing a beginning sentence and part of another that gave some structure to her complex stance toward Jaspers and the case of Angelo Cacci.

After working on her introductory sentences for 5½ minutes, Liz went back to the case study and began to gloss it. (She had originally only underlined it.) "It's from this sort of stuff that I get my best ideas." She was asked why, then, she did not begin her 60 minutes by performing this interpretive glossing. "I don't know," she answered.

As Liz moved through the last third of the hour, she continued reading the case study closely, following line by line with her finger, glossing every tenth line or so. At one point she commented, "Well, maybe he [Jaspers] is right," only to return to her original skepticism several minutes later: "All he [Jaspers] is really saying is that you don't get to see the end of your work. That means all these terrible things?" Liz was asked again if she was any closer to a thesis: "I don't know. Can't tell. Because it [is] actually only an hour. You know, you can't exactly judge . . . [You can] never really tell what it is until you're halfway done." Queried about the continual conflict between her quarrel with Jaspers and the requirements of the assignment as she understood them, she replied, "I just really didn't think it out well enough."

Looking back over the 60 minutes, three things about Liz's composing behavior are evident: (1) she never truly resolved the conceptual/rhetorical problem presented by the assignment; (2) she did not map out her discourse in advance but planned in increments as she wrote; (3) she edited prematurely.

1. Though the assignment instructions required that Cacci's case be discussed in light of Jaspers' quotation, they also gave latitude to dispute the applicability of Jaspers' vision. Liz began interpreting and applying the quotation almost immediately, but was not able to come up with an approach and resulting thesis that would enable her to deal with her reservations and the assignment's broad requirements. It is possible that Liz began writing too soon; even though most of the writing she produced was glossing and notes, these could have constricted a free-flowing reflection on Jaspers' vision and Angelo's life. At several points in the protocol Liz reported needing a good deal of time to "boil down" her ideas—with or without pen and paper—before any sort of final draft is considered. The 60-minute limit perhaps forced her to record more of that boiling down than she normally would. According to her reports, she spends a great deal of time at home ruminating on an assignment, jotting down notes, smoking cigarettes (she smoked five during this 60 minutes), drinking coffee, and taking breaks to watch television. Only when a deadline is upon her does she force herself to churn out what has yet to be done: "What I usually do is start about 6:00 p.m. and it's due the next day. . . . Pressure helps me. . . . If I have spare time, I'll just end up thinking instead of actually writing. . . . I don't like to work continuously." The present assignment, of course, made extensive rumination impossible.

2. Liz did not plan her essay in advance. She made decisions about the direction and shape of her discourse incrementally as she proceeded. This approach led to discoveries as well as dead ends, most of which, however, were fragmented. Her inability to arrive at a satisfactory approach to the assignment led to a further problem:

Liz said she needed "a place to end up," a conclusion, perhaps to provide a focus, a termination point for her incremental planning style. The fact that such a conclusion never emerged most likely worked against the success of Liz's incremental planning.

3. It is important to keep in mind that while Liz was trying to conceptualize an approach to the assignment and while she was laying out discourse in increments, in small "chunks of information," she was also scrutinizing her prose. She edited her earliest written reflections as she produced them.

The Invoking or Denial of Functional and Nonfunctional Composing-Process Rules and Assumptions

Liz expressed a number of rules directly: "Writing has to be logical"; "You're supposed to read [what you've written] to see how it sounds"; "You're not supposed to have passive verbs"; "If you can singsong [your writing], it's not good stylistically"; "You can't start a sentence with 'says.'" Several more rules could be implied from specific composing behaviors and Liz's comments on them: Writing is not good if "it's not clear, vibrant prose"; School writing should not "be too colloquial"; Word choices should not be "too simple . . . too easy"; Writing is not good if it contains too many prepositional phrases.

Many of the above rules apparently came from an editing text Liz had read the previous year. But whereas the text advocates reducing the number of "to be" verbs and prepositional phrases in one's prose, Liz seems to have interpreted the rules more absolutely, or had them so interpreted for her by overzealous professors and teaching assistants. Several other rules could also stem from the text (e.g., Writing is not good if it's not clear, vibrant prose; If you can singsong your writing it's not good stylistically). The balance of Liz's rules possibly come from other, earlier texts and teacher comments: writing has to be logical; word choices should not be too simple . . . too easy; school writing should not be too colloquial; and the puzzling "you can't start a sentence with 'says'" (a rule that is related to Liz's injunction against the colloquial; at one point she equated "says" with colloquiality).

While a rule like "you can't start a sentence with 'says'" is a strange one indeed and "if you can singsong your writing, it's not good stylistically" is questionable, most of Liz's other rules are legit-

COLLEGE OF THE SEQUOIAS
LIBRARY

imate and could be functional if they were not invoked at so early a point in the composing process. A further problem with some of these rules emerged when Liz was asked what they meant; she didn't really know. Finally, though one should not automatically equate the language with which a rule is expressed with the manner of that rule's enactment, Liz did express a number of her rules with an absolutism that could suggest a dysfunctional rigidity—an absence of context, purpose, and audience qualifiers that turns heuristic guidelines into narrow injunctions.

Enactment or Rejection of Premature Editing

Liz was .6 of a standard deviation above the Premature Editing mean. (Her "Occasionally" response to "My first paragraph has to be perfect before I'll go on" pulled her closer to the mean, and as was seen, Liz did not dwell on her first paragraph, but shifted to glossing the case study and framing further "blocks of information.") Liz's other responses to items in the Premature Editing subscale ("Often," "Sometimes," "Almost Always") suggest that she does have problems with early editing, and the stimulated-recall study confirmed this. As was noted in chapter 2, questionnaire items were constructed to tap general manifestations of a behavior, process, or attitude, but the items are not numerous or multifaceted enough to tap idiosyncratic variations such as the grabbag of rules that lead to Liz's early editing. Still, Liz very clearly edited prematurely, composing with the aid of a number of rules—some absolutely expressed, some not fully understood—which are appropriate to determine the final texture of prose but which are very inappropriate when one is working out ideas in rough draft or simply glossing an assignment sheet. The result, as was seen, is not only limited production but an actual stymieing and even forgetting of one's thoughts.

Interpretive and Writing Strategies for Complexity

Though she could understand the Jaspers quotation and the case study and was achieving some success in structuring complex notions in possible topic sentences, Liz never did arrive at an overall focus and plan for her essay. She reported that she rarely outlines or writes some other form of structured plan before writing; rather, she often follows a mental plan and sometimes simply works out ideas as she writes. The last approach characterized her work on the

COLLEGE OF THE SEQUOIAS
LIBRARY

essay under consideration. But that approach was not successful. Perhaps Liz needed more time to think through the issues; the 60-minute limit forced her to write before she was ready, and, thus, the reader gets a stream of preliminary and protean thought. Pertinent here is Liz's questionnaire response of "Almost Always" to "It is hard for me to write on topics that could be written about from a number of angles." (This was the only Strategies for Complexity item she so answered. She was at the mean on this subscale.) This response suggests that though time might have been a factor here, Liz frequently has trouble formulating and structuring multifaceted topics. Given that difficulty, it is a little surprising that she continues to plan so incrementally, that she does not rely on lists, crude planning sketches, or even some form of outline. Her responses to queries about planning strategies are telling:

Researcher: You say it's difficult to organize and get all these associations straight, and yet it's interesting that you never work out any kind of outline.

Liz: I've tried that a couple of times. . . . It works on a specific kind of paper.

Researcher: What kind of paper?

Liz: It works on the kind of paper where you're supposed to . . . report on six or seven things, what somebody said, and that's easy.

Researcher: What kind of an outline did you use?

Liz: I just put [the points] in order.

Researcher: You mean number 1, number 2?

Liz: Yeah, 1, 2, 3, and then I tried to, well, I tried to do it like you're supposed to, with the 1 and the A.

Researcher: But for other sorts of papers, . . . you tend not to outline?

Liz: Sometimes if I've got a . . . real tough paragraph, I'll try and do it for that one paragraph.

Researcher: Does that help?

Liz: I don't know. . . . I think it's probably a pretty good tool. It's just that I don't know how to use it. . . . I wouldn't know how to outline something [in a way] that would benefit me.

Researcher: Didn't . . . grammar school teachers teach you an outline form?

Liz: Well . . . they didn't tell you why you put in I, A, B, C, . . . It's like a research paper where they . . . tell us "O.K. write a research paper of about 12 pages." And the way they told us to do it was just to get quotes and string them together. So this paragraph is from this book. This paragraph is from that book. This paragraph is from that book.

The above excerpt suggests that Liz does not rely on pen-and-paper structuring and focusing aids because she does not have them in her repertoire. The outline she knows (but claims not to fully understand) is the old standard. She does not possess other techniques (such as, for example, those discussed by Linda Flower) that are flexible and suited for generating and guiding complex discourse.[2] In a sense, then, she lacks the quintessential strategy for complexity: an aid to balancing intertwining or conflicting issues. Perhaps this lack explains why she plans in increments, in "blocks of information" not unlike the disconnected quotations in her research paper analogy.

But Liz has read a lot and written a lot; though not a distinguished English major, her work is competent. It is possible, then, that though she cannot articulate a variety of planning strategies, she might well possess them tacitly.[3] If this is so, is there any other reason to explain her affinity for non-pen-and-paper strategies? The protocol offers one possibility, a belief in unstructured discovery: "I do believe that most of the time there is an answer to a question. And if you . . . start out a paper without really being aware of that [fact] and just say 'Well, I'll just go through this structure . . .' [you think] you've answered the question [but] you haven't. You've just kind of skirted around it." Her logic might be odd, but Liz's belief is fairly clear: structure a paper in advance and you do not truly penetrate a question and might not arrive at the best answer. Earlier in the protocol, Liz had noted that when she is interested in a paper, she wants to "let it say itself." A similar advocacy of the spontaneous is implied above. Perhaps this belief contributes to Liz's use of incremental strategies. And perhaps her inadequacy as a pen-and-paper planner determines the belief. But whether Liz's planning style results from inadequacy or preference or some interaction of the two, the result is the same, pithily expressed by Liz at the end of the protocol:

> *Researcher*: It sounds like sometimes you don't really know what [your paper] is going to look like and what it's going to be about until you're fairly long into it. Is that correct?
> *Liz*: Yeah. Cross your fingers.

Conflicting Rules, Plans, Strategies, and Assumptions

As was noted, a number of Liz's rules conflicted with each other at specific instances of composing—e.g., a particular line is good because it is rhythmic but bad because it contains a prepositional phrase, the prepositional phrase, of course, adding to the rhythm of the sentence.

More global conflict existed between Liz's need for extended pre-writing time—"boiling down," as she called it—and her premature editing. Premature editing also conflicted with her belief in spontaneity and discovery. How can one freely explore and uncover when one is assessing each word?

The Evaluation of Writing and Attitudes Toward Writing

Liz's negative evaluations of her writing were always aimed at specific phrases and clauses: "that sounds bad"; "that's really bad, bad writing." These evaluations were connected to one or more of her many rules—e.g., the latter evaluation was a reaction to prepositional phrases in the sentence: "Jaspers attributes the personal unhappiness of people like Cacci to the noncreative nature of their jobs." Note the overreaction. The sentence is not as lean as it could be, but it certainly is not "bad, bad writing."

Though Liz mentioned several times that certain English teachers made her conscious of aspects of her writing, she never voiced concern over the evaluation of others. If Liz's concern for others' evaluation is expressed at all here, it is manifested covertly through her embracement of her professors' and textbooks' rules.

Liz was asked if she enjoyed writing. She replied, "Sometimes, sometimes I do an awful lot." Asked why she concerned herself so much with editing on early drafts, Liz said she likes "monkeying around": "People always tell me . . . you should write your first draft . . . just do it . . . but I always enjoy the process of it." Liz also seems to like the play of ideas that accompanies composing: "Sometimes . . . I start thinking about something else that I find interesting, and I stop and think about that for awhile." Though writing does not come easy to her, Liz enjoys it, enjoys tinkering with language and exploring ideas. The videotape graphically displays this involvement: Liz bent over the page, her hand measuring out language; Liz sitting back, reflective with lit cigarette, only to snap her fingers, blurt "Ah ha!" or "That's it!" and quickly return to the page.

Discussion

It was recognized in chapter 2 that some high-blockers would be identified by the questionnaire Blocking subscale but would fall outside the identifying criterion (1 [or .8] standard deviation from the mean) for other subscales. It was also suggested that such writers, if videotaped, might well reveal complex idiosyncratic composing behaviors, processes, and attitudes that would account for their blocking. Liz was chosen because she fell 1.88 and 1.4 standard deviations above the means respectively on the two behavioral subscales, Blocking and Lateness, but registered less than .8 of a standard deviation on Premature Editing (.6), Complexity (.05), and Attitude (.1). In fact, her protocol did reveal the suspected process idiosyncrasies. She, for example, fell only .6 of a standard deviation above the mean on Premature Editing because, to the degree one can generalize from the present study, she seems willing to abandon a first paragraph before it is "perfect." Otherwise, though, she does edit prematurely, and with an array of rules to which the questionnaire at its present level of generality, could never be sensitive.

So Liz reported herself a high-blocker and, in fact, during the study, produced a very short draft. But why did she block? It seems for the same reason so many people block, from undergraduate to student lawyer to professional novelist—a thorny problem is confronted and cannot be solved, in some cases cannot even be clearly conceived. In Liz's case, she faced a point of view (Jaspers') with which she, during most of the session, could not agree. Furthermore, she had to carry out an analysis with that point of view. Undergirding Liz's dilemma is what Linda Flower and John Hayes have labeled the rhetorical problem.[4] How does a writer convert an assignment's request into an appropriately "elaborate construction" (p. 22) that both honors the assignment and allows the writer to exercise his or her beliefs and abilities? Though she finally framed a topic sentence, the protocol revealed that the assignment's rhetorical problem was one Liz never solved.

But Liz's difficulties did not begin or end with the above dilemma. Though she might have purely and simply been stuck intellectually, a number of factors made it all the more difficult (even impossible) for her to become unstuck, for her to solve her particular rhetorical problem:

1. It seems likely that the 60-minute deadline forced Liz to write

before she was ready. She might have needed more of the "boiling down" time she reported relying on at home. If Liz's composing at home is significantly different—temporally and qualitatively—from her composing in this study, then her troubles could be chalked up to the pressures of a 60-minute parameter alone and little more need be said. But, though unconfirmed self-report, Liz's composing in the present study was, in her words, "The way [she] do[es] it at home." She obviously gives herself more than 60 minutes (thus has more "boiling down" time), but then her assignments are considerably longer (I saw some of them), and she allows herself limited time to complete them. Why place such restrictions on herself? "Pressure helps" her push away the jumble of notes, the ruminations and diversions, and push toward the writing desk. "The way I do it at home" seems to refer to daydreaming, the generation of disjointed notes, pauses for cigarettes, coffee, and whatever else, battling deadlines and sometimes losing (remember, she was 1.4 standard deviations above the Lateness mean), and limited, sometimes stymied production.

This is not to say that the deadline was not responsible for Liz's writing before she had her thoughts clarified; it is only to suggest that her thoughts might often not be formulated before the clock forces her to begin writing the kinds of segmented notes produced in this study.

2. Another factor interfering with Liz's composing is her paucity of planning strategies. Certainly, pen-and-paper plans, as Janet Emig and others have shown, are not prerequisite to good writing,[5] but for Liz's incremental planning style to be effective she would need both a sense of academic discourse (with Liz's senior status in English, this can be assumed) and a fairly unconfounded, though even general, notion of what one wants to say (Liz lacked this). She set out, trying to frame "blocks of information" when either freewriting (which she preferred not to do) or outlining or sketching (which she claimed not to know how to do) might have freed up, possibly clarified, her thinking. She was left with few alternatives with which to solve the rhetorical problem she confronted—she could ruminate, generate her "blocks of information," or return to reading and marking assignment materials, but that was it. Her options were limited—no freewriting, no heuristics, no sketches or outlines.

3. Perhaps because of the 60-minute pressure but also perhaps because of habitual composing behaviors, Liz was fairly unmethodical in her approach to the assignment: she knew "boiling down" helped her, but she dove into writing "blocks of information" and attempts at topic sentences. The result? "I really didn't think it out well enough." She also knew glossing helped her "get her best ideas," but for reasons she could not pinpoint, she did not begin glossing the case history until the hour was half over and until she had attempted topic sentences.

4. Still, other students compose without the aid of plans and with jumbled ideas and in unmethodical ways and yet sometimes write themselves out of their conceptual jungles, even under the pressure of 60-minute essay exams. (See, for example, the upcoming case of Glenn.) But the final stymieing touch for Liz was her concentration on verbal surface—concentrating on the minutiae of surface even before a fundamental confusion about topic was resolved, even while glossing assignment materials in search of ideas.

The question that must be forming by now is "Why doesn't Liz know better?" She is a senior English major in good standing; she must have learned more about writing than the scramble of factors presented above would suggest. But before one begins questioning Liz's abilities, several facts need to be pointed out.

a. Liz holds a set of assumptions and preferences that could undergird her planning style, her unmethodical approach to composing, and, to some degree, her premature editing. She advocates a fairly spontaneous approach to composing and distrusts carefully plotted attempts to compositionally solve problems. (Though she does believe in mulling over, "boiling down," issues involved in the assignment.) She also gets pleasure out of "monkeying around with words" and toying with ideas, apparently at the expense of production and, occasionally, at the expense of deadlines.

b. Liz's embracement of so many rules—often to the detriment of her fluency—seems odd unless one considers her situation. She had been told by several teachers to read an editing text; that would, the teachers putatively claimed, rid her of some nagging wordiness problems. Now, the textbook is wittily and forcefully written; it would take a fairly self-assured student to ignore it. What is more, the confusion Liz evinced vis-à-vis textbooks and teacher injunctions could reflect conflicts between the graders she encounters: "They said, 'Don't use "I."'" But those have always been the papers

I've gotten the best grades on. . . . When I use 'I,' they give me an 'A,' and when I don't, they don't." A pilot study by Gary Sloan and a more extensive piece of research by Rosemary Hake and Joseph Williams suggest that faculty can champion one standard and grade by another,[6] so Liz's statement, if accurate self-report, might not simply be unfounded complaining.

Liz never could resolve the conceptual and rhetorical problem presented by the assignment, for, as was seen, a number of process barriers and possibly a deadline stood in her way. It seems she should know better, and there might be reasons other than cognitive ones to explain why she does not, but, as her protocol comments suggest, she holds to certain assumptions and finds herself in certain situations that seem to interact with each other and with aspects of her composing process in ways that pretty convincingly impede her fluency.

A Low-blocker: Glenn

Glenn is a sophomore Theater Arts major with a 600 VSAT and a 3.85 GPA. His writing experience placed him in category 6. He received a score of 23.75 on his essay. His questionnaire results follow: 1 standard deviation below the Blocking mean; .4 of a standard deviation below the Lateness mean; 1.1 standard deviations below the Premature Editing mean; .9 of a standard deviation below the Strategies for Complexity mean; .9 of a standard deviation below the Attitude mean.

Glenn's Essay

Several elements of Jaspers' quote deal directly with Angelo Cacci's case. Cacci's loss of caring for his girlfriends, his view of his job as "O.K.," his history in general all seem to point to a lack of commitment. And without commitment there can be no continuity in reference to the man of modern times and his job. The job is performed and then forgotten. This relates directly to Cacci's view of his job as "O.K." He is noncommital about it. He probably has no feelings about it. It is only a way to get a few bucks and pay the bills. Angelo won't say "I hate it, but I need the money." This would require employment of an emotion. It seems Angelo has forgotten emotion. This is further exampled in the fact that he won't say he was in love with his girlfriend. He further discounts the relationship by comparing it to a past girlfriend. "I've been through this before," he says, relegating his feelings for the girl to something commonplace, unexiting.

As Jaspers claims that modern man lives a life of ephemeral activities—he builds a product and moves on to something new without a second thought—so Angelo lives his life without thought or emotion. He is a near robot. He has been at his job for ten years, has a good employment record, and, if he were to stop and look at his work, would probably realize that he is bored stiff. But as Jaspers says, Angelo—modern man—won't or can't look up from the machine long enough to see what's going on.

Angelo says that his relationship began O.K. with his girlfriend, "but after a while it fizzled. I just didn't feel that much for her anymore." He couldn't retain any emotion for her. He probably became afraid of what he was feeling, afraid to let any emotion into his life. Or perhaps he began to feel there was no point in expending the energy required for the relationship. Perhaps the answers to why he acts as he does are in his past—who knows? But his biggest problem, as Jaspers says about modern man, is that his life has no continuity. The only thing that is constant in Angelo's life is his lack of caring, his apathy toward his surroundings. He can't make any commitments.

Angelo's dream seems to illustrate his view of himself as non-commital. The dog that is injured in his dream is aided not by him, but by another man. "Love for things and human beings wanes and disappears," as Jaspers says. Maybe Angelo feels he should help the injured dog, but he doesn't. And through acts like these in his real life, ultimately his love and feeling for things dries up and vanishes.

A great deal of speculative answers to Angelo's problems can be drawn from his past—his mother's gradual growth into a spiritless t.v. freak, his father's leaving—and perhaps these facts are important in determining Angelo's present lifestyle. But Angelo must ultimately be made to realize that he possesses a brain and a heart and is not merely an "element of an apparatus," as Jaspers claims. Angelo must see that it is wrong to avoid emotion, to block out feeling, or one becomes divorced from oneself. He must seek, in Jaspers' words, "an expansion of the selfhood."

Glenn's Session

Overview. Given his attenuated composing time, Glenn was the most fluent writer of the 10 students. He did not begin writing until

11½ minutes into the hour and finished 12½ minutes before the 60-minute deadline. Though he paused 72 times during the 36 minutes of his composing, 24 of those pauses lasted five seconds or less. Only three pauses exceeded one minute. Glenn's longer pauses tended to come at the beginning of paragraphs as he thought through the direction of his discourse; once past those foundational sentences he wrote quickly, pausing briefly as he poured out two and three sentences at a time. He did not appear rushed, but rather at ease, assured, in control.

During the first 11½ minutes of the session, Glenn read and reread the materials; though he was "looking for things that the two sources have in common," he did not mark the Jaspers quotation or case history in any way. Glenn would eventually arrive at a solid understanding of Jaspers' vision and Angelo's situation, but that understanding did not come without some difficulty. Five minutes into the hour he was "just really confused": "I was trying to think of something to . . . connect it all together. At this point I don't know. It seemed really fragmented to me." Through the second five minutes of the hour, he unsuccessfully shifted his attention once again to the case history: "I was trying to get a general line of thought in the essay and I wasn't finding it, actually. This whole thing about his past, and then all these things about the girlfriends and his present life." And the quotation turned out to be more broadly philosophical than the kind of material he was used to working with:

> *Glenn*: Again I think I am just trying to tie in what I've just read, what I have gathered from the . . . case study . . . I am looking for this quote to be a concrete, matter-of-fact thing.
> *Researcher*: And it's not working out that way?
> *Glenn*: No. He is saying things like, "His life has no continuity." "What he does has no purpose."
> *Researcher*: That's pretty broad?
> *Glenn*: Yes. Just general ideas.

Glenn's expectations were thrown. He had more experience analyzing "really concrete" prose to which he could readily apply a standard five-paragraph pattern: "I remember this diagram that they drew for us a million times; there is the inverted triangle [on top] and then three rectangles and then the triangle at the bottom."

As he neared the 10-minute mark, Glenn did not have the thesis he could readily present (the inverted triangle) or the three points from which three paragraphs (the three rectangles) could be generated. He became conscious of the time. How to start:

> Some times I just think, "All right, what I'm going to do . . . is just start writing and it will come." [Other times I think,] "No, I am going to search until I find a really good starting point that I am really confident of and go from that." And that is what I am doing right now is deciding which of those to use.

But after 10 minutes of reflection, an approach began to gel:

> I think it is starting to come together, what I think the person who wrote the question wants. I am looking to the question. Specifically, "Does Jaspers' passage shed any light on Angelo's situation?" It is starting to come generally that Angelo is the modern man Jaspers is talking about.

At this point, the introductory phrase of Glenn's first paragraph ("Several elements of Jaspers' quote") "just popped into [his] brain," and he began writing, choosing to commence writing with a general direction but not with "a really good starting point."

Glenn then paused for 23 seconds ("Now I am thinking, 'Well, O.K., let's name the elements'") and wrote his second sentence, looking back at the case history to make sure he was not forgetting any major points. As he was writing the second sentence ("Cacci's loss of caring for his girlfriends, his view of his job as 'O.K.,' his history in general all seem to point to a lack of commitment"), Glenn "just wanted to spew [the three topics] out, get them out and see where I could go from there," but was also aware that what was emerging would set him up for three paragraphs: "Right now, that is running through my brain, that classic essay pattern that I have."

The next three sentences came quickly. At this juncture, Glenn became concerned about "whether the things I was writing were really just the way I am feeling right now in my life . . . or whether they were really actual connections between the two [passages]." At first he worried about the evaluators' reaction, "but then I quickly got rid of that and wrote the way I wanted to." Still, at points throughout composing he expressed mild concern about his penchant for possibly subjective interpretation. ("I think it is the big problem with the whole paper.") Therefore, he often worked in a reference to or quotation from Jaspers or the case history, "trying to get it back to the factual."

The next seven sentences, hastily written, all short and rhythmically repetitious, developed by description rather than by analysis Glenn's contention that Angelo views his job with little emotion. Asked about the speed of the writing here, Glenn replied:

> When I'm through, when the idea is finally washed out of my brain and onto the paper, and I feel safe that I am not going to lose it by putting in the punctuation, then I go back and put it in . . . I just really want to get the ideas out and just go, go, go with that, and something good will come out of it, and then [I'll] go back and worry about whether it's grammatically perfect or not.

Glenn's next statement revealed a self-assurance that undergirds his willingness to conceptually sprint through his essay and worry about grammar later: "I think I am confident enough about my abilities and grammar . . . that, you know, I feel safe enough that I can go ahead and just get all the ideas out and then worry about that."

But several sentences later, Glenn wrote, "He further discounts the relationship by comparing it to his"; he stopped, crossed out "his" and continued, "an older girlfriend." Glenn paused briefly, crossed out "older" and substituted "past." Questioned about what could be seen as a contradiction to his "go, go, go" injunction, Glenn explained: "I was thinking that the reader would interpret that as a girlfriend who was older than him . . . 'his' made it sound like it was his only girlfriend. He had two girlfriends." So while Glenn does not seem to be concerned about grammatical infelicities as he writes, he is very much concerned with even a single word's effect on his reader and does not leave the change, in this case anyway, for some after-the-fact editing period. Perhaps reader response (to a display of verbal prowess) is also behind the one other time Glenn stopped to ponder a single word. While composing the last sentence of paragraph one, he stopped after the clause "relegating his feelings for the girl": "I just really drew a blank. I started looking back at the word 'relegating.' I really like that word. . . . [But] I was looking back at it thinking 'it doesn't fit . . .' then I drifted off." After a 1½ minute pause, a phrase "just came and it sounded really good to [him]." The phrase ("to something commonplace, unexciting") allowed him to "use relegating in this sentence."

About to start paragraph two, Glenn again voiced concern "that I am not really connecting the two sources" and thus resorted to one of his favorite cohesive devices—a reference to Jaspers ("As Jaspers claims"). Throughout this paragraph, Glenn will oscillate between what he terms "the factual" and the expression of his "own feelings." He veers off, at times repetitively, into his own response to Angelo's situation, but continually pulls himself back to the texts with transitional phrases ("But as Jaspers says") or with direct quotations. Glenn discussed a similar but more conceptually elaborate technique while viewing the production of the sixth and seventh sentences of paragraph three. The sixth sentence grants a possibility, but the seventh expresses another point of view, one, by the way, that ties the discussion once again to Jaspers and cohesively back to the first paragraph's notion of absence of continuity: "That was another element of that perfect essay. In your first paragraph, you address the pros, you address the cons of the issue. You directly address what people might say against your topic, and you try to disprove them. Then you go on to what you feel . . . that is what this is, even though it comes at the middle of the paper when it would usually come at the very beginning."

Glenn's first attempt at a fourth paragraph resulted in an optimistic interpretation of Angelo's dream. Though Glenn deleted only three words in his first three paragraphs, he deleted this entire paragraph after finishing it and rereading the case history. (This was, by far, the largest deletion made by any of the 10 students.) "This paragraph's not too bad," he observed, "[but] it turns out to be totally wrong . . . when I read the dream the first time, I thought, 'an element of hope here,' . . . but I went back . . . and it doesn't show that at all." Glenn can express personal and, as one reader put it, "self-indulgent" views and then tie his discussion back to Jaspers and Angelo. But here he apparently transgressed some personal standard of objectivity and appropriateness. His second version of paragraph four—one that offers a bleaker interpretation of Angelo's dream—seemed more accurate to him: "The paragraph I wrote before . . . I must have known wasn't true, and that's what made me go back and read it." But Glenn's revision should not be seen as evidence of a deeply felt commitment to one point of view. He was pleased that though the original paragraph was "totally wrong," it was still "not too bad . . . which is one thing I like about my writing." Asked to elaborate, he explained: "I don't need a total commitment behind my writing . . . I could write on something that I did not really feel strongly about."

Beginning his last paragraph, Glenn was "trying to decide . . . whether there is anything new I can bring in . . . 'Is it time for a conclusion, or is there anything else I can bring up?' And, I am bored." Queried on how he was going to approach this conclusion, Glenn explained: "I am looking for one more really strong point, and I did not find it. So I wrote . . . a sort of tying-up of the ideas, addressing what maybe were the answers. That is another option to restating all of the old factors with no new ideas. That is what I did here—offer possible solutions to the problem." Asked if he learned his problem/solution approach when he learned his "classic essay pattern," Glenn said: "That is an option that I have adapted. I don't think they want us to do that in . . . this little ideal structure for an essay . . . It probably came out of that twelfth grade class [self-expressive writing] that I had . . . which [encouraged] getting your own ideas into the paper a little more." These deliberations resulted in Glenn's longest pause—three minutes and seven seconds. But after composing his first sentence, Glenn became concerned about violating his "little ideal structure": "I was thinking about the fact that I am not supposed to be bringing in any new ideas according to that ideal essay—God, I can't believe I still retain that thing—but I go ahead and do it anyway because I like the flow of what I'm writing." Having made his decision to follow the success of emerging production rather than an abstract ideal, Glenn produced two more sentences interrupted by five pauses. Then, while composing his fourth and final (and most rhetorically effective) sentence, he paused for 22 seconds:

Glenn: I was really aware of ending with a quotation because that is another thing I have learned somewhere along the line. You never end with a quotation. You always end with your own words. Your interpretation of a quotation is all right, but you never end with a quotation.
Researcher: Then why did you end with a quotation?
Glenn: Because it worked. It just worked there.

Glenn finished the sentence, smiled, and wrote "The End" at the bottom of the page. He did not proofread, though during each third of his composing time he did pause to reread several sentences or more of previous production: "I almost never proofread a paper . . . I feel this purging when I write—this 'get it all out, it's all done, I don't want to look at it anymore'—and I just hand it in."[7] Asked if he meant he was a one-draft writer he said "yes" and added: "They tried to get me into [rewriting] in high school . . . we would turn a paper in, get it back, do another draft, and turn it back in. I think I just did not see that many results or much change. I don't know how to rewrite is probably the problem. I don't know how to do it. I don't know how to go back over something and make it work better."

But though Glenn could probably present his much-considered audience with a more appealing essay if he proofread and revised accordingly, he is still a facile and effective—if somewhat unfocused and self-indulgent—student writer. At the end of the session I asked Glenn about writer's block; he answered with an assurance that characterized his composing: "I can't really remember a time when I sat down and it was like, 'My God! I don't know what the hell all this is.' Whereas my roommate does that all the time. So does the guy downstairs. It freaks me out. What's the problem. 'Here are all the sources. Let's go kids. Write!'"

The Invoking or Denial of Functional and Nonfunctional Composing-Process Rules and Assumptions

Glenn has a multioptional rule to direct him when facing the blank page—at times he "just starts writing and it will come," at other times he waits for "a really good starting point" before composing. The demands of the writing situation seem to determine which option he follows. In the present case, he used both: he thought through the assignment until his initial confusion was resolved ("Angelo is the modern man Jaspers is talking about") but waited no longer and began, working out a firmer direction through the first half of paragraph one.

In two instances, Glenn mentioned rules (Don't introduce new ideas in the last paragraph; Don't end the last paragraph with a quotation) but rejected them because they ran counter to the success of what he was producing. (In the case of the first rule, Glenn also had past instruction that encouraged him to question the rigid five-paragraph structure, though, it will be recalled, not without some conflict.) This rejection of rules in the face of success suggests, though this is conjecture, that Glenn composes with a high-level "meta-rule" which directs him to consider the context and effectiveness of his writing before acting on text or teacher rules. A statement of his suggests that such a rule might reflect something essential in his personality. "That is pretty much my attitude about everything. To hell with it if it does not work."

Three other rules, though not directly stated, can be inferred from repeated behaviors and protocol commentaries. One grants priority to getting ideas on paper rather than to grammatical correctness. Another gives the reader a central role in the composing process. The third is a complex, apparently flexible rule that directs a balance between personal observation and fidelity to assignment materials. The rule also presents options for maintaining fidelity: transitional references to authors, direct quotations, etc.

Enactment or Rejection of Premature Editing

Only one time in the protocol did Glenn concentrate on verbal surface to the sacrifice of his thought. The word "relegated" stumped him, and he drifted into reverie. Otherwise, both his behavior and his previously cited commentary gave precedence to ideas hitting paper. Felicities can be taken care of later. (And, in some cases, not at all, for while Glenn might have proofread sporadically, he did not do so methodically.)

Glenn's confidence in his grammatical skill could be an important variable here. Perhaps some such assurance frees writers up, allows them to concentrate on ideational substance, knowing all the while they can later clean up their flow of ideas. Certainly the reverse is true. Sondra Perl found that her basic writers were so concerned about their grammatical skills that they could not produce a single sentence without stopping a dysfunctional number of times to judge the correctness of their language.[8]

Interpretive and Writing Strategies for Complexity

Glenn completed the essay with the aid of three effective strategies: an interpretive strategy that sought similarities between Jaspers and the case study, an organizational strategy that resembled the five-paragraph pattern he learned in high school, and a development/cohesion strategy, loosely adapted from argumentation, that resulted in a "granted this, but that" pattern within paragraphs. But Glenn did not gloss his materials in any way, and that absence of strategy (given his further reluctance to generate a written plan) might have negatively affected the organization and development, though obviously not the fluency, of his essay by making information somewhat inaccessible to him as he composed.

Pertinent to this study was Glenn's strategic flexibility. This flexibility was manifested in three ways.

1. Glenn "sometimes" makes outlines but, confused as he was during the session's first 10 minutes, decided not to: "I was looking at the information, and I was thinking that an outline wouldn't help me with this." Instead, he waited until he saw a connection between Jaspers and Angelo and then began to write, working out "a substitute for an outline" in the second sentence of his essay.

2. Though Glenn referred to his "classic essay pattern" three times in the protocol, he modified it as he brought it to bear on the assignment. He did not build inductively to a thesis—placed last— in his introductory paragraph; he did not refrain from bringing in new information in his conclusion. He modified or abandoned these characteristics of his "ideal essay pattern" as his barriers and discoveries demanded. (This does not mean to say that his adaptation was expertly effected. He failed to adequately explain all three of his subtopics within his first paragraph, and he [I would guess inadvertently] did not develop those topics in the order presented in sentence two.)

3. In discussing his adaptation of a "pro-con" technique from his "ideal essay pattern" (and, in fact, he might be confusing two essay modes here—the expository and the argumentative), Glenn explained that the technique "would usually come at the very beginning" but that he needed it within the essay to bring him back to "the factual." Though Glenn might be working with a confused pattern, the important thing is that he can veer from it, modify it as need dictates. Again, this does not mean that his adaptation is without flaw. Though he competently executes his pro-con strategy at the sub-paragraph level, the entire essay seems to embody an argumentative thrust that is not really grounded in concrete opposition and never truly gels. It might well be that the argumentative approach allowed Glenn to best deal with the rhetorical problem presented

by the essay. The way he solved the problem allowed him to bring an effective pro-con strategy to bear on his intra-paragraph fluctuations between personal indulgence and factual accuracy, but he was not able to expertly turn the entire discussion into solid agrument.

Conflicting Rules, Plans, Strategies, and Assumptions

Glenn's protocol was free of any conflict. This was surprising, given the number of disparate rules and plans he mentioned. What is important, though, was that Glenn's rules and plans—as he expressed them—either embodied alternatives or were subject to situational exigencies.

One other potential conflict not mentioned above and only alluded to in the Overview was the possible clash between Glenn's concern for audience and his predilection to "get the ideas out and just go, go, go." A concern for audience could stymie some student writers, forcing a hyper-scrutinizing of every sentence generated. This was the case with one young woman in my pilot study, "Rigid Rules."[9] But whereas she did not seem to have a clear notion of what her audience wanted or of how to integrate concern for audience into her composing process, Glenn seemed to have both a feel for his audience and an ability to use his audience awareness to aid his composing choices: "I had a really great idea in my brain, but I was feeling, 'Hum, this sentence isn't really getting my ideas out . . .' I guess I think a lot about the person who is going to be reading this paper. I try to think of the voice I am creating in the paper for the reader. . . . It gives me a really good focus which is really important when I'm writing." With the possible exception of Glenn's conflict over "relegating," his awareness of audience served to guide rather than block the flow of his prose. It did not force him to anxiously ponder the effect of every phrase.

The Evaluation of Writing and Attitudes Toward Writing

Glenn was very much aware of audience reaction to his work and several times expressed concern about reader response to his self-indulgence. (Though once he quickly countered his concern and "wrote the way [he] wanted to.") But, on the whole, he was pleased with his writing and assumed his reader would be as well.

As for Glenn's attitude toward writing, his questionnaire responses to "Even though it is difficult at times, I enjoy writing" and

"I like having the opportunity to express my ideas in writing" were "Often" and "Almost Always," respectively. Yet, as was discussed earlier, Glenn can detach himself from his prose, almost, one feels, with a touch of cynicism. ("I could write on something that I did not really feel strongly about.") This does not mean to say that Glenn will write anything with equal abandon; as was seen, he felt better about a new, more accurate, fourth paragraph than about a falsely optimistic original. Asked about the motive for this revision, he replied, "I am interested in my own mind." Still, "I am just really lazy, most of the time, in my writing. I go a lot for what will sound good and sometimes it works. Usually it works." Asked why he thinks he seldom blocks, he replied, "I will settle for second best."[10] . . . Sometimes I feel like people can't really tell if it is the second-best idea . . . look at those papers I wrote in high school—all those A's." Glenn is a competent writer who has been reinforced for his efforts and who gets some pleasure out of exercising his skill. But his investment of personal energy stops there: "I don't feel my expository writing is going to be the way I ultimately want to express myself. It is not really that important to me."

Discussion

Both readers had some positive things to say about Glenn's paper, and the average of their scores yielded the study's third highest evaluation. But the readers also pinpointed some obvious flaws: the treatment of Angelo and Jaspers, in one reader's words, "tends to be repetitive, to fail analytically." The essay never pulls its argumentative edges together. Development falters at several points. Infelicities and awkward constructions occasionally mar the prose. Perhaps the essay would have been tighter if Glenn had glossed his materials and attempted some sort of written plan. Perhaps the infelicities and awkward constructions would have been caught during careful proofreading. Whatever the case, Glenn did not make best use of his prewriting time nor did he proofread. His essay is intelligent but flawed. But it was produced quickly, displays fluency, and is relatively effective.

It would be difficult to deny that one explanation of Glenn's facility can be found in his lucky combination of competence and absence of self-imposed pressure. He is willing to settle for less than perfection because expository writing is "ultimately" not the way he wants to "express himself." (It turns out that songwriting is.) Taking what Glenn values into account, one still cannot deny the importance of the rules he has that spark production and offer context-dependent alternatives and the importance of his ability to abandon potentially rigid rules when he sees that they run counter to the flow or effect of his discourse. Also important are his planning and discourse strategies and his ability to extract, modify, and apply techniques from them. One could easily imagine a student who shared Glenn's attitude toward academic exposition but who lacked the linguistic skill and/or the cognitive flexibility that enabled Glenn to succeed as he did.

It seems as though Glenn's fluency and adaptability are rooted in two not unrelated high-level concerns: the importance of displaying his mental facility and his interest in the reaction of his reader. Though Glenn effects a certain distance between himself and his page ("I could write on something that I did not really feel strongly about"), it is important to him that what he writes is not "totally wrong" and that he balances his "subjectivity" with "objective" elements from an assignment's materials. He seems to take pride in his ability to produce academic writing. It seems, as well, that Glenn is very concerned with sounding intelligent, with weaving discourse that cleverly connects to a clever reader. This ultimately rhetorical concern significantly influences his composing: he won't edit prematurely because it might interrupt the flow of his thoughts. He won't hold to rigid rules like "don't end your last paragraph with a quotation" because they will subvert the felicitous effects he's creating. He'll adapt a strategy like the give and take of argument if it seems effective in its new guise. Glenn might well hold to fundamental assumptions about school writing that are not all that different from the rhetorician's assumption that discourse is a social act.

4

Conclusion

Summary of Results

Identification of High-blockers and Low-blockers: Questionnaire Reliability and Validity

The statistical analyses summarized in chapter 2 suggest that the writer's block questionnaire is a reliable instrument; that is, it evokes relatively consistent responses. But a questionnaire can be reliable but not valid—people can respond to items with some consistency, yet the items might not be measuring what they're purported to measure. One indication of the validity of the writer's block questionnaire was presented in chapter 2. The multiple regression analysis demonstrated a positive relationship between the Blocking subscale (the major behavioral indicator of writer's block) and the remaining cognitive/behavioral and cognitive/attitudinal subscales. I also conducted a further test of validity by comparing the questionnaire responses of the (admittedly small) subsample of 10 students chosen for the stimulated-recall study with that subsample's subsequent comments and behaviors during stimulated recall. These students' comments and behaviors almost uniformly supported earlier questionnaire responses. In the handful of instances where comments and behaviors seemed to contradict earlier responses, further investigation removed or explained the contradiction. An example: Ruth, a high-blocker, fell one standard deviation above the Premature Editing mean, yet did not edit prematurely during the study. It turned out, however, that during the quarter that had elapsed between questionnaire and stimulated recall, she had worked with a teacher who disabused her of "rewriting before writing."

A word of caution: Though there is good reason to believe that the questionnaire is reliable and valid, its limitations (discussed in chap. 2) must be kept in mind. The items in the Blocking and Lateness subscales are broadly behavioral and therefore would probably serve to identify most high-blockers, but the remaining items focus on the cognitive, and on a subset of cognitive functions at that. The questionnaire, then, like any diagnostic instrument, should be used primarily as an initial screen. What it suggests about individual students must be confirmed and elaborated through more comprehensive investigation.

Rules

Protocol analysis revealed that low-blockers expressed 17 times as many functional rules as did high-blockers, and one-quarter of the nonfunctional rules. All low-blockers seemed to function with rules that imply "if this . . . then that" enactment. That is, contextual options appear to be a dimension of the rules' operation (e.g., if Dana discovers or recalls new information while writing essay exams, she will hurriedly insert it; given the relaxed time of a take-home paper, she'll rewrite her paper to better accommodate it). Several low-blockers also voiced, then rejected, rules that, had they been enacted, would have countered successful composing (e.g., Glenn, contrary to rules he had been taught, introduced a new idea in his last paragraph and concluded the paragraph with a quotation "because it worked"). High-blockers, on the other hand, simply did not express or imply many rules that embodied the above contextual flexibility.

All low-blockers expressed rules and prompts that sparked fluency (e.g., "When stuck, write a few words"; "I just really want to get the idea out"). Three of the six high-blockers also voiced such rules and prompts, but the prompts were either simple, nonalternative goals uttered in face of a deadline or rules which were countered, even conflicted, by other rules, assumptions, or inadequacies.

Two of the six high-blockers expressed rules with rigid absolutism (e.g., "If you can singsong [your writing], it's not good stylistically"; "You're not supposed to have passive verbs"), and this rigidity seemed to limit their production. One of these two students (Liz) even tried to enforce rules she did not understand. The only rules stated absolutely by low-blockers were a few functional ones (e.g., Amy's interpretive rule, "It does no good to highlight everything, because everything is not that important").

Assumptions

Three of the high-blockers (Liz, Ruth, and Terryl) voiced assumptions about how writing *should* occur. These assumptions elevated the spontaneous and seemed related to a rejection of formal, pen-and-paper planning. (Terryl even termed such planning "diabolical" because it ran counter to the honesty of immediate expression.) Significantly enough, Liz and Ruth, and possibly Terryl, in this case, seemed to need the prefiguring and direction pen-and-paper planning can sometimes provide. None of the low-blockers voiced absolutistic assumptions about how writing should go; rather, three of the four (the fourth, Dana, was a relatively inexperienced—that is, category-one—writer) seemed to take the assignment and flow with what emerged as they wrote. Ironically, they were in many ways more spontaneous than their blocking peers. It is possible that, for some students, an avowal of the spontaneous limits planning options and thus makes them in some ways less spontaneous than the writer with a repertoire of strategies.

A fourth high-blocker (Gary) held to an overblown and thus limiting assumption: there are infinite ways to say anything and the slightest variation between one way and another will result in totally different reader responses. Gary interpreted the assignment and composed his draft in a very analytic and cautious fashion. The foregoing assumption could explain his composing behavior.

In brief, none of the four low-blockers stated absolutistic assumptions that channeled them into narrowed, interpretive planning or composing styles. Four of the six high-blockers did.

Premature Editing

As I reviewed the protocols, it became clear to me that everyone, to some degree, edits from first thought to final sentence. It is the frequency of such activity that determines premature editing. Low-blockers circumvented premature editing three times as often as did high-blockers and engaged in it half as frequently. (A circumvention occurs when a writer avoids premature editing via some mental strategy or behavioral trick. An example would be the student who circles a misspelled word with the intention of returning to it once she has gotten her thoughts onto paper.) Varied data suggest five, not unrelated, causes of premature editing; one or more of them, especially in an additive way, seem sufficient to lead a writer to edit too early. (1) Lack of confidence in one's mechanical/grammatical skills. At the opposite end of the spectrum from Sondra Perl's error-vigilant basic writers[1] is a low-blocker like Glenn who explained, "I feel safe enough that I can go ahead and just get all the ideas out." (2) Certain planning styles. Data from earlier versions of the questionnaire yielded low, but significant, correlations between planning styles that did not rely on pen and paper and Blocking and Premature Editing.[2] Planning styles will be further discussed momentarily. (3) Single drafting. Terryl, a high-blocker, gives perfect expression to the possible relation between writing only one draft and scrutinizing verbal surface: "I write with the thought . . . that this is going to be it . . . so it had better be good the first time through." (4) Certain rules and assumptions about language and composing. Recall here Gary's assumption that slight variation in language leads to major differences in reader response; the assumption seemed to lead him to an exceptionally overcautious composing style. (5) Attitudes toward composing, particularly in the school setting. Dana (a relatively inexperienced writer who did not block) forges through considerable skill limitations partially because she sees an essay as another assignment that must be completed. Terryl and Liz, two high-blockers who are far more skilled at and enamored of writing than Dana, enjoy "monkeying around" with language or finding the "perfect word" but, in this case, to the detriment of their fluency.

Paradoxically, some of these posited causes are not without merit. English teachers, for example, would give their pedagogical eye teeth to get students "monkeying around" with language. But simple fluency cannot be overlooked. When a writer fixes himself on surface features—on correctness or the perfect phrase—the thinking process might not be allowed to run its course.

Strategies for Complexity

Interpretive Strategies. All students displayed interpretive strategies. Undoubtedly because of the nature of the topic and the setting, writers did not approach the assignment pell-mell. Certainly some strategies were more sophisticated and more effective than others, but the one clearly inappropriate set of interpretive strategies was exhibited by a high-blocker. Rather than proceed with his general understanding of the materials, Gary analyzed those materials so thoroughly and atomistically that he produced unwieldy amounts of data. His case suggests that blocking can be rooted in processes that prefigure writing, in the ways students prepare information for composing.

Planning Strategies. Several high-blockers evinced difficulties that seemed to arise because they planned incrementally; that is, they didn't think through and/or write out any approaches before beginning their drafts, but planned in increments as they wrote. The protocols suggest that for incremental strategies to work, certain requisite abilities and behaviors should be present: (1) a knowledge of the discourse frame the student is working toward, (2) a facility with "cohesive ties," particularly transitional expressions, (3) rescanning, (4) a solution to the rhetorical problem a particular assignment embodies. Not all incremental planners displayed these abilities and behaviors. To complicate matters, some planned incrementally because they knew of no other way. Such incremental planners-by-default are truly in a bind; they are using a strategy for which they do not possess the prerequisites, yet cannot shift to other, possibly more appropriate, strategies. Two of the low-blockers wrote without the aid of traditional plans, but did not plan incrementally. Glenn, modifying a classic five-paragraph pattern, constructed a plan within his first paragraph; and Stephanie seemed to build three underlined phrases in Jaspers into a simplified plan that, while not honoring the complexity of the assignment, did streamline that complexity, thus enabling her to write. The other two low-blockers relied on somewhat more traditional written plans. One of these students was a category-one writer, and her planning seemed to aid her fluency in the face of significant strategies for complexity problems. The foregoing data suggest that incremental planning, especially when that is a student's only option, can lead to difficulties, for its effective use presupposes a number of abilities and behaviors all undergraduates do not display. This contention supports Linda Flower and John Hayes' call for training in planning[3] and counters some self-expression/discovery advocates' disdain of formal planning.

One of the findings reported in "Rigid Rules" was that some students blocked because they tried to compose with inflexible planning strategies. Such inflexible planning was clearly evident in Gary's case. After meticulously analyzing the assignment's instructions and materials, he began to condense all the resultant discoveries of his analysis into a long list of topics which he then attempted to further condense into a topic sentence. As a result, he was unable to produce more than abortive leads into an essay he couldn't finish. But Gary was the only one of the six high-blockers to display such a dramatically narrow strategy.

Several case studies also suggest that a dimension of flexibility might, paradoxically, be a storehouse of forms normally thought to be fairly inflexible (like the five-paragraph essay) from which the student can work and which he can modify and even choose to ignore. The studies do not provide insight into how such flexibility is learned and operates.

Writing Strategies. Once the actual writing of the draft was underway, low-blockers evinced twice as many sentence-to-essay level strategies as high-blockers and were in need half as frequently. Oddly enough, the high-blockers on the whole were a more experienced group; three were upper-division English majors. What seems likely is that their lack of sentence-to-essay level strategies is in some cases attributable to the binds and conflicts they experienced. Observing high-blockers, then, one might note a lack of strategies due to limited repertoire or due to complex process dysfunctions. The two causes might not be easily distinguishable—an example of how process problems can confound the display of competence.

Conflicting Rules, Plans, Strategies, and Assumptions

On the average, high-blockers were conflicted eight times as often as low-blockers. In the few instances where low-blockers did experience conflict, the conflict was over local semantic/rhetorical issues (e.g., Amy couldn't decide if she should begin her first sentence with the assignment's phrasing or with words of her own choosing). These conflicts did not last long. High-blockers' conflicts (and all but Terryl expressed them) were much more global, or, if local, were plentiful and pervasive. Low-blockers expressed *potentially* conflicting rules and plans. But what is telling is that these rules and plans tended to embody alternatives, options that could be variously enacted as the writing situation demanded. Thus conflict was averted.

Attitudes Toward Writing

High-blockers voiced about 1½ times as many negative evaluations of their work as did low-blockers. Most of these evaluations were specific, were leveled at a word, phrase, or sentence that violated a rule or criterion. The direction of these tabulations supports the study's conceptualization of writer's block, but are not as striking as other tallies. And other than the above, there are few notable attitudinal/evaluative differences between high-blockers and low-blockers. On the average, the two groups are fairly equal in their approval of their productions and in their conceptions of approval or disapproval by others. These data do not support popular notions that writer's block is primarily a manifestation of low opinion of one's work and fear of evaluation.

Attitude seems more related to ability than to blocking. The subscales Lateness, Premature Editing, Strategies for Complexity, and Attitudes correlate .37 to .59 with Blocking, and much lower among themselves—with one exception. Attitudes correlates .47 with Strategies for Complexity. (Attitudes correlates .44 with Blocking.) Of the 10 students, those who had the lowest Attitudes scores and, during stimulated recall, who voiced the most frequent, occasionally global, negative evaluations were the two category-one (i.e., least experienced) writers—a high-blocker and a low-blocker, both of whom were over one standard deviation above the mean of the Strategies for Complexity subscale. Some high-blockers, as the case studies revealed, liked to write very much, and, though high-blockers did level more negative evaluations at specific productions than did low-blockers, the ratio was not all that disproportionate. Writer's block, then, cannot simply be blamed on a nagging internalized parent or critic.

The Balance of Thought and Action

As with the solving of any problem, there seems to be a highly individual point in composing past which cogitation becomes if not dysfunctional at least counterproductive. Not simply is fluency affected, but the solution of substantive and structural problems is potentially held at bay, for such problems are often worked out as the writer writes. Some seemingly reflective writers might be more entangled in rigid rules and conflicts than engaged in fruitful thought. As compared to low-blockers, high-blockers on the average spent 9.1 more minutes (of their 60-minute composing period) pausing, and two high-blockers devoted one-half to three-quarters of their 60 minutes to prewriting and planning. The result was that only 15 percent of the words these two students produced appeared on the drafts they turned in. A further result was that they received the readers' two lowest evaluations.

Three of the other high-blockers reported a similar imbalance in the way they allotted time to composing, but in the present study were impelled by the deadline. Whereas a deadline can arouse anxiety in some (and did so in Ruth, resulting in a flurry of disconnected sentences), and have little effect on others, it seemed to help these three students push aside some rumination, uncertainty, and limitation and get pen to paper. In Terryl's case, skill was displayed sufficiently to earn him the readers' second highest evaluation. Still, the three students evinced enough problematic behavior to give some indication of what their composing is like when the deadline does not loom.

Earlier I suggested that high-blockers and low-blockers are defined as such by the way they compose within the constraints of school writing assignments. The simulation created in this study suggests that low-blockers function more efficiently than high-blockers within these constraints. Much of their efficiency seems rooted in their repertoire of flexible rules and appropriate plans, their goals to produce first and refine later, and in their general absence of conflict. Compared to high-blockers, they are able to effectively balance thought and action, to efficiently allot their time to interpretation, planning, and composing.

Implications for the Model

In chapter 1, I presented a sketch of a composing-process model. In light of the study's data, the model can now be reconsidered and fleshed out. Each of the model's components will be discussed in turn—with one exception. The study did not include a methodical examination of the ways a writer stores, retrieves, and prepares the propositions that comprise her knowledge base, so that dimension of the composing process will not be treated.

The Executive: Composing Styles

Theories of cognitive style suggest that human beings do not process information in a uniform way; some tend to deal with certain kinds of information impulsively, others reflectively, some serially, others holistically, and so on.[4] No test of cognitive style was given to the students in the present study, but case-study data revealed sufficiently different approaches to composing to warrant speculation on a notion possibly related to cognitive style—composing style. The model holds that writers do not envision or approach writing in the same way. The reason for this variation could lie in the nature of executive-level, problem-solving strategies and assumptions—the way they are conceived, organized, weighted. For example, a particularly methodical writer might possess a general interpretive problem-solving strategy that states something like: "To understand an assignment, break its directions into component sections, then analyze each of those sections." He might also hold a composing assumption that states something like: "Good writing proceeds step by step." These and other executive-level strategies and assumptions could combine to form a general orientation to composing—a composing style.

Case study data suggest at least three composing styles:

1. The ruminative style (the writer is reflective, ponders linguistic and ideational choices, is given to lapses of thought, is easily captivated by an idea or by the play of language).

2. The analytic style (the writer is cautious, precise, prefers a focus on particulars of language or process rather than on the entire writing task).

3. The pragmatic style (the writer tends to make interpretive and compositional choices in light of the purpose of the task—the writer looks outward to audience).

A particular style might predispose students to internalize certain rules, planning styles, etc., rather than others, and might also predispose certain students to fluent vs. relatively strictured (though not necessarily blocked) composing—e.g., the ruminative writer might tend to produce discourse slowly, the analytic writer might tend to get caught up in sentence-level particulars at the expense of broad discourse goals.

I want to underscore how tentative this speculation is. Research on cognitive style, though extensive, is problematic. And it would be foolhardy to base a notion as comprehensive as composing style on a single study like the present one. But if a series of studies could demonstrate that composing process differences maintain over a broad cross-section of writing tasks, then the impression one gets from some composition textbooks that all students learn to write or can be taught to write or actually do write in the same way would be seriously challenged.

The Executive: Composing Assumptions

It seems that a writer's assumptions are very much related to the composing subprocess options he follows. In the present sample, planning styles, particularly, seemed influenced by the writer's notions about spontaneity, creativity, and personal integrity. Premature editing was, in part, traceable to one high-blocker's assumptions about linguistic encoding and decoding. And several low-blockers' adaptability was either rooted in or mirrored by beliefs that elevated rhetorical usefulness and audience need. These relationships suggest that assumptions could be powerful (truly "executive-level") influences.

Composing Subprocesses: Rules

With the exception of certain kinds of prompting rules (e.g., "When stuck, write a few words"), rules that set boundaries to composing activity (e.g., "It does no good to highlight everything, because everything is not that important"), and rules of convention (e.g., "Indent a paragraph"), it seems that a functional composing rule is not simply a directive, but, rather, a complex mental statement that somehow contains considerations of context and purpose. Functional rules embody situational alternatives, are more involved than the algorithmic rules of mathematical operations. Functional composing rules are flexible, multioptional. Rigid composing rules are enacted acontextually.

Blocking can result if too many of a writer's rules are limited-alternative directives. (Or too few are multioptional.) The play of her ideas is attenuated; the rhetorical decisions she can make are restricted. This is not to say that every rule in a writer's mind should be nonabsolutistic and multidirectional; prompting rules, boundary rules, and rules of convention are most likely "rigid." Theoretically, blocking could also occur if a writer's every rule contained options; the unrelenting decision-making would be overwhelming.

Composing Subprocesses: Interpretive Plans

The assignment a writer faces elicits an interpretive plan, a way to render the task and its materials accessible for composing; only the careless, uninitiated, unskilled, or anxious writer approaches school-writing helter-skelter. But the kinds of interpretive plans that emerge can be very different. The 10 writers in the present study all wanted to find correspondences between the case history and the philosophic excerpt, yet their interpretive strategies ranged from a quick, unmethodical, nonscribal attempt to spot a few associations, to a methodical glossing of the case history with categorizing references from the excerpt, to a painstaking, atomistic scrutinizing of every sentence in the excerpt.

Not surprisingly, the most effective interpretive plans were appropriate to the constraints and specific demands of the task. This finding implies that effective interpretive planners possess a wide array of planning options, and their choice of option includes consideration of the nature of their writing task. As for using or bypassing pen and paper as an interpretive aid, there seem to be two related considerations: (1) The writer's familiarity with both the kind of writing and the issues the task presents—the more familiar, the more he can rely on purely mental strategies alone. (2) The length of the task's materials and the writer's memorial capacity. But it seems likely that as length and complexity of task and materials increase, even the most extraordinary of interpretive planners would have to be aided by some means (like underlining) of highlighting information.

Blocking can occur during this first phase of composing if the writer's interpretive strategies are inappropriate to the task; that is, if his interpretive activities yield too little or too much information for the task at hand or yield information in a way that makes it inaccessible—e.g., those students who interpreted the case history in terms of their personal experiences were stuck when it came time to render that history for a Jasperian analysis. Blocking can also occur if the student relies on memory beyond his capacities.

The foregoing suggests that some university students' problems in interpretation might not lie in understanding the task itself but, rather, in taking the next step. Given a particular task, what interpretive strategy—from underlining and listing to paraphrasing and classifying—is most appropriate? The protocols of the 10 students in this study suggest that some undergraduates possess limited interpretive strategies, and thus their problems begin before they even start their drafts.

Composing Subprocesses: Writing Plans and Discourse Frames

One unexpected outcome of the protocol analysis was that incremental planners experienced a number of difficulties. The model did not predict that any planning style—from sketching and outlining to developing discourse in increments—would predispose a writer to block; as was suggested in "Rigid Rules," the flexibility of the style's enactment would be the key variable. But as I noted while discussing the conclusions of this study, a number of conditions are necessary for the incremental style to be effective. The incremental planners in this study did not display the conditions necessary for success; they planed incrementally because they knew of no other way, because the plans they did know (e.g., the traditional outline) were envisioned in too static and unmanipulatable a fashion or because of powerful assumptions about composing. These students' behavior suggests that certain planning styles might not result from individual preference and cognitive predisposition as much as from the limitations of one's planning repertoire. Their behavior also suggests that writer's block (and other composing problems) can result not only from planning inflexibility but also from the absence or limitation of ancillary conditions necessary to certain planning styles.

The protocols also revealed the plans and discourse frames one would expect to find in university writers of even limited skill: sentence-level syntactic and intersentence cohesive patterns, paragraph-to-essay structures, various discourse modes with the traditional intentions to explain or persuade. What varied, of course, was the students' sophistication with each of these. But what emerged as well were unexpected planning/discourse strategies: for example, a linear presentation of concepts and an almost spatial orientation to the presentation of information. These strategies have not been catalogued in rhetorics or textbooks and lead one to wonder how many planning/discourse frames actually exist in the real world of writers writing. On the other hand, both strategies could be adaptations—forged as the writer needed them—of more fundamental, familiar strategies: narration in the case of the former and description in the latter. Such adaptations were more clearly seen in other protocols—e.g., the scaling down from essay to intersentence level of the classic "granting the opposite" argument strategy; the modification of the standard five-paragraph essay pattern to suit particular needs. These adaptations do not necessarily lead to quality writing, but they do seem central to fluid composing. Only low-blockers displayed them. This adaptability suggests that low-blockers possess an array of flexible strategies or patterns and, during the act of composing, can manipulate them to suit emerging composing needs. What is important to note, though, is that while some writers could adapt other frames and strategies to the present task, such adaptability did not guarantee the creation of a frame and strategy completely appropriate to the task at hand. It is currently popular to talk about students creating form out of a need to express deeply felt content; the present limited data suggest that form will indeed be created by (fluent) writers, but the form might not be adequately complex to satisfy the conceptual/rhetorical demands of the task. This implies that forms, patterns, and frames are not created ex nihilo, but are adapted from what a student knows. If a student's repertoire of frames is limited, the complexity (but perhaps not the fluency) of his discourse will be limited.

Composing Subprocesses: Attitudes

While the study suggests that there might not be a strong association between the expression of positive or negative evaluations and a collegiate writer's fluency, several case studies raise the possibility that one aspect of the evaluative process might be integrally related to fluid or stymied production: the criteria used in evaluation. Earlier I suggested that some writers might block because they match their production against unattainable, and thus inappropriate, models. Evidence of this inappropriate comparing was not found in the protocols, but what was revealed was that both category-one writers (the least skilled—one was a high-blocker, the other a low-blocker) could not always explain why they made the compositional choices they did, nor could they readily explain how they judged the effectiveness of their choices. These evaluative shortcomings seemed to slow them up, confuse them, or lead them to mislabel their writing problems. Certainly, a writer does not have to articulate, say, grammar rules in order to produce grammatically sophisticated sentences. But, if one can extrapolate from the admittedly limited evidence provided by two students, it seems that writers need to have evaluative criteria of some kind stored in some fashion against which they can judge their compositional options. These criteria will usually not be expressed in textbook fashion; they will be expressed idiosyncratically, even awkwardly, but they will be available to the writers just the same. Since evaluative criteria were most poorly articulated by the category-one students, one could hypothesize that criteria problems might be more related to blocking in lower-skilled students than in more advanced writers. At higher-skill levels, the writer simply has more experience with his medium and has been taught or has personally appropriated more criteria to aid him in choosing and judging.

If the reader will grant the importance of accessible criteria in the evaluative process, I would like to posit two further refinements: (1) Not all criteria problems are of the same caliber. Criteria related to diction choices are probably not as potentially stymieing as criteria related to broader organizational or thematic issues. (2) As with other variables discussed in this study, criteria problems alone might not cause a writer to block, but criteria problems interacting with other variables (e.g., planning style) could lead to strictured fluency.

Opportunism

Though the model proposed earlier posited opportunism as a fundamental characteristic of composing behavior, that early stage of the model did not present any set of processes to account for opportunistic activity. After reviewing the protocol data, I can say with some assurance that fundamental to opportunism is a repertoire of strategies, rules, plans, frames, and, possibly, evaluative criteria, and the richer the repertoire the richer the opportunistic activity. Writers cannot opportunistically shift strategies if they have little to which they can shift. It also seems likely that, given this repertoire, the primary cognitive prerequisite of opportunistic behavior is that strategies, rules, plans, and frames be flexible and multioptional, be conceived conditionally, embody alternatives. Rigid, inflexible strategies, rules, plans, and frames restrict the play among top-down, bottom-up, or "horizontal" movement from one option to another, and thus restrict the writer's ability to take advantage of emerging compositional possibilities. Conflict represents a particularly dramatic stricturing of opportunistic behavior, and, again, a key element in conflict seems to be limited flexibility in a writer's strategies, rules, and plans. Low-blockers voiced potentially conflicting rules, but their rules seemed to embody conditions and contextual alternatives.

The interaction of a writer's executive operations, composing subprocesses, knowledge base, and emerging text is phenomenally complex; freeze any given moment of his composing, and this interaction could be characterized as being primarily top-down or bottom-up or horizontal, and also as primarily rigid or flexible. But over the course of writing, fluid composing would be characterized by oscillation between the deductive and inductive, the occasionally rigid and the more-often flexible. The more alternatives a writer has, the more fluid his rules and plans, the less likely he is to block—the more he can opportunistically work away from dead ends and exhausted possibilities.

Implications for Instruction

On first thought, it seems that an Implications for Instruction section of a book on writer's block ought to contain a list of techniques, even tricks, by which teachers could free up stymied writers. But simple techniques won't necessarily get to the heart of what impedes a writer and most certainly won't contribute to pedagogies that will help forestall the problem. For example, one simple self-engineering technique for people who over-edit is to write all early sketches and drafts in journals, notebooks, or on scratch paper. Composing in this fashion reminds writers that they are not preparing final copy. While such techniques undoubtedly work for some writers, they won't work for others. It is important here to recall that Liz, the high-blocker most fully described in this study, was editing prematurely while glossing her assignment's passages on the assignment sheet, clearly not a piece of paper she would submit. We don't have reason to believe that having Liz write on notebook rather than looseleaf paper, or crumpled rather than smooth paper, would do much good. Her problem is too complex.

I'll devote this section, then, to speculations on ways we teachers can forestall certain process problems and to suggestions for diagnosing the process problems our students have already developed. I don't want to imply that various techniques and tricks might not prove handy. My message is that the teacher or tutor should resort to them only after a true understanding of a particular student's difficulties has been reached. For those wishing a description of techniques, I can recommend two sources: Mack and Skjei's *Overcoming Writing Blocks* (Los Angeles: Tarcher, 1979) is a nice compendium of advice and procedures ranging from tips on how to relax before writing to techniques that aid revising. Peter Elbow's ninth chapter of *Writing with Power* (New York: Oxford, 1981), a highly imaginative guide to invention, provides a wide variety of techniques for the stymied writer. The chapter is aptly titled "Metaphors for Priming the Pump."

Diagnosing Process

We spend a great deal of energy diagnosing our students' writing skills. The present study suggests that we should also spend time exploring their writing processes. We simply can't tell enough from finished essays alone. (And, of course, objective measures tell us next to nothing.) A striking example of the limitations of product analysis can be found in the case of Ruth, one of the study's high-blockers. Ruth got anxious while writing her draft and sped up, producing a long, rambling paper that was peppered with allusions and insightful connections, but that was also repetitive and disjointed. The experienced readers who evaluated her paper said some accurate things about the draft's difficulties, but also labeled Ruth's style "arrogant" and "swaggering" and surmised that "the student [is] taken with [her] own sense of prowess." Ruth's stimulated-recall commentary revealed a very different compositional/rhetorical reality. What was labeled as "swaggering" was, in fact, the result of anxiety rather than of arrogance, and with this knowledge is easily read as being "uncertain" rather than "swaggering." Furthermore, the anxiety (combined with other factors) contributed to some unusual and counterproductive composing behaviors. But imagine Ruth submitting to a teacher a draft like the one she produced for this study. If the class was fairly well along, the teacher would know that Ruth is not a student taken with her own prowess. But the teacher would not necessarily know how Ruth's process went awry, and thus not have much of a clue as to how to intervene. And, of course, if Ruth visited a tutorial center with her paper, the tutor, possessing much less history on Ruth than a teacher, would be at an even greater disadvantage.

Both teachers and tutors, then, need to investigate process as well as product. Let me present three, increasingly powerful, ways to gain entry to process.

A good deal of process information can be uncovered by conducting writing history/writing process interviews with individual students. Teachers and tutors would want to do this early on. Here's one way to proceed: Have the student save and bring every scrap of paper used for a recent assignment—the less time lapsing between composing and interviewing the better. Begin with general questions about previous writing courses, academic and nonacademic writing activities inside and outside school, attitudes toward academic and nonacademic writing. (If a formal survey of writing attitudes and processes is desired, see Daly and Miller's questionnaire,[5] or my questionnaire, which is presented in app. A.) After this general questioning, turn to the student's written work. Examine all scraps and drafts. Point out specific features (e.g., a list or scratch outline, words crossed out or inserted, elements clearly absent—for example, no evidence of planning) and ask simple questions (e.g., "Where did you learn to outline this way?" "What word did you scratch out? Why?"). If the student's responses conflict with earlier general statements, gently question the contradiction. The student's answers might reveal more accurate information—earlier statements might have been the result of theorizing rather than accurate reporting of behavior. Of equal importance, fundamental conflicts between assumptions about what one should do and what one actually does might be uncovered. Thus the interview proceeds, the teacher or tutor avoiding judging and elaborate theorizing while focusing the student continually on specific text features. (More refined procedures and instruments for analyzing the writing process can be found in *Assessing Changes in Composing* by Lester Faigley, Anna Skinner, David Jolliffe, and Roger Cherry of the Writing Program Assessment Project at the University of Texas at Austin.)

These post-hoc interviews can be enlightening, but, as I suggested in chapter 2, such questioning suffers from the fact that memory fades quickly. A somewhat more effective procedure would be to have the student compose in front of the teacher or tutor. If the observer can put the student at ease, a good deal of information could be garnered. The interviewer's questions would still come after the fact, but soon after the fact. Many composing choices would still be fresh in the student's memory. Of course, the teacher could actually interrupt composing at salient moments—long pauses, for example. Such interruptions can provide rich information but should be done sparingly. The more interruptions, the more derailed a writer can become.

Muriel Harris, Director of Purdue University's Writing Lab, has attempted to gain even more immediate access to composing processes by adapting for tutorial assessment the researcher's technique of speaking-aloud protocol analysis. She has the student speak aloud while composing, audiotapes the session, and plays it back. Thus she and her student can pinpoint specific process problems. As I noted while discussing the relative merits and limitations of various research techniques in chapter 2, not all students can be guided to speak aloud while composing, and those who can will be composing under unnatural conditions. Still, the speaking-aloud technique reveals a remarkable amount of information, and to insure validity this information can be checked against students' written products and other accounts of their composing processes.

What to do once information is garnered? Remedy problematic assumptions and rules and supplement sparse strategies through conferences and tutorials, through lessons, readings, CAI programs, and through modeling and small group work. I have further general as well as specific suggestions, and those will be spread throughout the remainder of this section.

Enhancing Conceptions of the Composing Process

As this study suggests, many of our students have developed narrow or distorted conceptions of the writing process. Elsewhere I have speculated that some causes of such inaccurate conceptions might rest in composition textbooks and in our profession's insistence on product correctness (over other dimensions of discourse) and our research and training institutions' narrow definitions of writing skills.[6] Whatever the causes, our students' misconceptions profoundly affect their growth as writers. Fortunately, the new wave of process pedagogies provides some broad assurance that students will be offered richer images of what goes on in a writer's mind, and the spread of conferencing and peer-editing approaches promises increasing insight into the writing processes of self and others.

Still, I would strongly urge teachers to spend time discussing and revealing the intricacies, idiosyncracies, and rich complexities of composing. One series of pedagogical strategies: Give students excerpts from interviews with professional writers who exhibit diverse approaches to invention, planning, and revising. (The *Paris Review* series, *Writers at Work*, is a rich source. One provocative pair of authors would be Georges Simenon and Jack Kerouac; another less dramatically contrasting pair are Vladimir Nabokov and Ernest Hemingway.) Present students with facts from manuscript studies— e.g., that E. E. Cummings revised some of his playful, seemingly simple poems well over 100 times. Reveal facts about our own composing processes. Some teachers like Donald Murray even compose in front of their students.

Though conferences and peer groups provide numerous insights about process, we need to make sure that such information doesn't get lost, is somehow systematically shared. My UCLA colleagues Faye Peitzman and Jim Williams rely on several different procedures to assure this sharing: they give their students writing process surveys and/or have them observe and report on their processes. Extending Peitzman's and Williams' approaches, we could even have our students become novice researchers, the focus of their mini-projects being their own writing processes. They could speak aloud while composing (at school or home), tape what they say, and transcribe interesting segments. If tape recorders are not available, they could observe and interview each other using post-hoc or speaking-aloud techniques. Finally, we could expose them to the composing processes of students who might (but might not) be worse off than they are: give them, for example, a segment of Liz's case study—perhaps where she's editing prematurely or having trouble planning. It strikes me that, particularly for remedial writers, it could be very valuable for students to gain some distance from the composing that can so ensnarl them and come to understand how composing can go awry.

Please understand, I am *not* suggesting that we turn our courses into composition T-groups and endlessly spin the cotton candy of our own mental complexity. I am suggesting that we take some time to educate students and let them educate us and each other about the composing process. How else will we find out what lies behind the faint noise of their scribbling pens? As important, how else will they begin to demystify their own processes? And with demystification, true education begins.

What would such education yield? Three general results, the first and second at first glance paradoxical:

1. An awareness of the rich functional individual differences in composing.

2. An awareness of certain general realities that seem to hold for most writing. An example: One's best writing does not necessarily come fully formed· even the brilliant, seemingly spontaneous performance (e.g., the verse produced by the Renaissance poets who donned the mask of sprezzatura; Kerouac's three-day sprint through *The Subterraneans*) is built on slowly acquired technical virtuosity, prethinking, and rehearsal.

3. An awareness of counterproductive procedures.

These three goals combined would do a lot to forestall or correct the sorts of misleading assumptions and counterproductive behaviors revealed in this study.

Rigid Rules: The Absence of Context

One of the most dramatic differences between this study's high- and low-blockers is, in some ways, the least surprising: the presence or absence of rigid rules. The teaching, practice, and receiving of writing has too often and too zealously been reduced by English professionals and the larger culture alike to the teaching and envoking of rules. Rules, particularly absolute or simplified ones, make a complex process less mysterious and threatening. Many of our less able writers constantly ask us for rules so as to dispel their uncertainty, and, as Mary Vaiana Taylor's study of teachers' attitudes toward usage has suggested, we teachers might react to insecurity about language by resorting to absolutes.[7] (How comforting it feels, especially in an academic setting, to rely on the authoritative wit of Orwell or E. B. White or Jacques Barzun.) And the problem occurs not simply with grammar and style. The composing process itself is often reduced and simplified in textbooks because it is too complex a process to be presented in its multifaceted richness.[8] There are all sorts of reasons, then—psychodynamic to sociological to cognitive—to explain why rules have become synonymous with composing. Unfortunately, the rules are often represented in rigid, absolute, narrow ways. As we've seen, rigid rules focus the writer's mind too narrowly, don't allow him to work effectively with the large issues of the writing task. They also skew his linguistic and rhetorical judgments. True, writing—like any nonrandom intellectual task—is a rule-governed behavior, but, as this study suggests, the rules in the fluent writer's mind are, for the most part, multioptional and flexible.

Rules about grammar, about process, about style, about form should not be taught as dicta. Even nominalizations, passives, highly complex syntax, the abstractions Strunk abhors *can* have linguistic, psycholinguistic, rhetorical, cognitive justification.[9] We teachers of English must teach rules appropriately—that is, as propositions about writing that have a history and a sociology and that are contextual, that are appropriate in some cases and not appropriate in others, that, in short, are dependent on the aims of discourse and are not themselves the aim of discourse.

I will offer a few suggestions on the teaching of propositions about writing through the course of this section, particularly in the last several pages. The teacher interested in reading discussions of certain of the grammar and usage rules we take as absolutes can begin with the following accessible and enjoyable articles and books: Irene Teoh Brosnahan, "A Few Good Words for the Comma Splice," *College English* 38 (Oct. 1976): 184–88; Charles R. Kline, Jr. and W. Dean Memering, "Formal Fragments: The English Minor Sentence," *Research in the Teaching of English* 11 (Fall 1977): 97–110; Elizabeth S. Sklar, "The Possessive Apostrophe: The Development and Decline of a Crooked Mark," *College English* 38 (Oct. 1976): 175–83; Jane R. Walpole, "Why Must the Passive Be Damned?" *College Composition and Communication* 30 (Oct. 1979): 251–54;

Richard A. Lanham, "The Abusage of Usage," *The Virginia Quarterly Review* 53 (Winter 1977): 32–54; and Jim Quinn, *American Tongue and Cheek* (New York: Pantheon, 1980).

Interpreting Assignments: Reconsidering Invention

Several high-blockers submitted extremely limited final drafts partially because they set out to interpret the study's assignment in counterproductive ways. Gary comes to mind with his procedures that generated myriad data and endless lists. While discussing implications of this study for a cognitive model of composing, I noted that the most effective interpretive plans seemed to fit the demands of the study's writing task. If that observation can be generalized beyond the confines of this study, it has important implications for the way we teach students about prewriting and invention.

Some current invention strategies like brainstorming and freewriting encourage the student to generate material without constraint. Certainly there are times when such fecund creativity is helpful. But I suspect that the more prescribed a task is, the less effective such freewheeling strategies might be: the student generates a morass of ideas that can lead to more disorder than order, more confusing divergence than clarifying focus. Perhaps fairly circumscribed tasks would better be approached with more defined, though still general, heuristics: Aristotle's topics or Burke's pentad or the Tagmemist's particle, wave, field framework. And recently, composition specialists have developed heuristics for more specific purposes: for example, heuristics for expressive and persuasive writing and for helping the writer envision audience.[10] None of the writers I observed, either in pilot or final studies, relied on any of the foregoing heuristics, so I have no empirical base from which to speculate on their relation to fluency or blocking. Such heuristics would seem to aid the stymied writer by encouraging a focused production of ideas. But my examination of inflexible strategies in high-blockers also leads me to believe that any heuristic (for heuristics are strategies) could be inappropriately reduced to an inflexible grid, as constraining as the most static outline. And, too, any heuristic can be misapplied. (Christensen's generative rhetoric, for example, would not work well with many abstract expository tasks, though it can be a powerful heuristic for descriptive writing.)

Heuristics and other invention/prewriting strategies are often presented as being equally applicable to all sorts of tasks. But if it is true that effective interpretive planners are skillful in matching their strategies to the specific qualities and constraints of a task, then one strategy might not be as good as another. Yes, the more strategies the writer possesses, the better. And it is definitely true that the strategies must be taught as strategies, as dynamic, flexible processes—which, of course, contributes to their applicability. But it seems to me that we teachers ought to show our students that the writing task and the writer's situation determine which (even flexible, multipurpose) strategy is most appropriate. How defined is the task? ("Write on a social issue that concerns you" or "Discuss vegetable imagery in 'To His Coy Mistress.'") How much does the writer already know? What are the task's length and time limits? What is the purpose of the task? (To evoke an expressive or more academically formal response?) Some of these concerns are basely pragmatic, others invitingly conceptual. But all are important, for they raise the *context* of the writing task and remind us that strategies are not envoked in some abstract and rarified dimension but in real environments with multiple constraints. We should teach students to match strategy with environment.

Planning for Writing

Theorists from Richard Larson to Linda Flower and John Hayes have made clear the need for instruction in strategically rich plans for writing. There is no need to repeat their thesis, only to support it: our students need a variety of flexible planning strategies, strategies that aid them in ordering complex information and that, in addition, hold the potential for aiding them in discovering information. The only point I would add here is that no one strategy is best for all students and all assignments. Individual differences of student and task must be kept in mind. Of course, the more strategies or variations of strategies a student knows, the more facile he is likely to be. Both in "Rigid Rules" and in the present study, low-blockers worked with plans that aided their fluency.

But my pilot studies as well as the present investigation reveal another dimension of the problem. It's not simply that students don't, loosely speaking, know strategies, it's that some of them don't truly understand the planning process. They learn a pattern (the classic outline or spoke outlines or Gabrielle Rico's cluster diagrams) but not the mental operations the patterns represent. It's as though they've memorized a mathematical formalism without understanding the mathematics it represents. It will be recalled that Liz knew that for "a specific kind of paper" (one, it seems, that pretty much calls for a listing of information) the classic outline might be useful. But she didn't quite see how to transfer the principles of the outline to other tasks; I suspect that the complexities of coordination and subordination, as reflected—at least in theory—in the classic outline pattern, were not entirely clear to her. (This is not to say that the pattern itself does justice to those complexities, only that Liz didn't seem to grasp and be able to transfer the operations the classic outline does represent.) A variation of this problem was manifested by Martha in "Rigid Rules." She could construct an elaborate process chart that did show the relations among disparate bits of information, but didn't seem to be able to make the bridge from her plan to an essay. The complex weaving became an end in itself; her plan did not lead outward to discourse. To continue the earlier mathematical analogy, she did understand the formalism but couldn't use it to solve problems.

Liz's and Martha's problems are not the same, but both suggest a disjunction between the processes and intentions of planning and the means we use to represent that process and intention. This disjunction helps explain the inflexibility of some high-blockers' planning strategies and suggests that we teachers must not assume competence in planning when we see our students scribbling out plans. We need to test that competence, particularly where planning for "higher-level" exposition is concerned, for that kind of discourse particularly requires an understanding of the relationships of abstractions.

One final thought. Three high-blockers questioned planning as being constraining, as limiting the spontaneous play of ideas. Earlier I suggested that such perceptions of planning could well be based on powerful assumptions. It strikes me now that these three students might also be reacting to the static, empty formulae that too often pass for plans in our classrooms and textbooks. Such advocates of spontaneity need to be shown that some planning strategies *are* fluid, aid in discovery, become ways of enhancing rather than restricting the play of ideas.

Not Structures but Strategies

There is no need to summarize the very large body of pedagogical theory and research on sentence stylistics, paragraphing, or discourse structures. What does seem warranted from this study's data, though, is a vote in favor of teaching patterns, structures, and frameworks. Such a vote seems odd, given the problems some of the high-blockers had with patterns and structures. I'll address this issue of constraint vs. flexibility in the last part of this section, but let me note here that low-blockers simply had more—or more flexible—sentence-level to broad discourse-level patterns at their disposal. (Of course, as I suggested earlier in this chapter, some high-blockers may have had rich repertoires of such patterns, but weren't able to display them because they were stymied by premature editing, conflicts, etc.) At the heart of some low-blockers' facility was the ability to adapt patterns that could be constraining. Glenn modified the standard five-paragraph pattern to suit his needs. I'm also reminded of Debbie, one of the fluent writers in "Rigid Rules":

> In high school I was given a formula that stated that you must write a thesis paragraph with *only* three points in it, and then develop each of those points. When I hit college I was given longer assignments. That stuck me for a bit, but then I realized that I could use as many ideas in my thesis paragraph as I needed and then develop paragraphs for each one.[11]

Debbie asked a teaching assistant if her modification was sensible. The TA said yes, she tried it out, and it worked.

What we must remember is that many of our student writers are hampered by a lack of sentence, paragraph, and discourse patterns with which they can present complex information. We must also keep in mind that as writers develop, there are often stages in their growth where they rely on narrow and simple patterns. The question is, are these patterns presented by teachers as rigid frameworks, as ends in themselves, or as structures that are to be built upon? From another perspective, are the structures taught both as structures *and* strategies, as approaches that can be varied as rhetorical need arises?[12] If they are, then it seems likely that there will be greater chance that students will understand that form is subordinate to intent and will be able to use these forms with some flexibility. From their reports, it sounds like neither Glenn nor Debbie was taught the five-paragraph pattern in this fashion. But both had further interactions with teachers (and perhaps both are fairly flexible problem solvers) that helped them modify an originally static form. Why not teach structures in such a way to begin with?

Attitudes Toward Writing

Among the issues potentially related to attitudes toward writing, the expression and application of evaluative criteria emerged as a process worth considering further. I indirectly dealt with some issues related to evaluative criteria when discussing assumptions and rules, for writers invoke these when evaluating their work. But worth further consideration are the manner and atmosphere in which students gain their criteria and the manner, in turn, in which they apply them. Are criteria applied rigidly, one-dimensionally, acontextually, without adequate understanding? Liz comes to mind. She dutifully (mis)applied a variety of stylistic rules while generating ideas, and some of the rules were rules she didn't adequately grasp. ("When [a textbook author is] talking about 'to be' verbs, I don't really even understand what he's saying.") In the way we discuss writing, particularly issues of usage and style, in the way we comment on student papers, in the models of good writing we present, do we encourage inflexibility and misapplication? And do we (or our books) convey such monolithic authority that some of our students will follow our word even though they don't understand it?

One implication of the above is that we should help our students understand why they say what they do about their writing. One way we can contribute to their ability to evaluate their work is to encourage them to discuss the reasons behind their compositional choices (or the reasons behind their judgments of others'—peers' or professionals'—work). Liz revealed the source of an editing rule as well as her confusion about it. A teacher or tutor could then help her better understand the rule and place it in its proper context and could further get her to reflect on why she follows a rule when she doesn't understand it.

We could also help our students come to understand that one applies different criteria to different phases of the composing process and to different kinds of discourse. They would see that, say, editing, is only one dimension of writing; therefore, the criteria one would use when preparing a paper for submission might be quite different from criteria one would use when generating ideas or writing oneself out of a conceptual tangle. If a student judges all phases of composing and all aims of discourse by a single set of criteria, then he will be evaluating narrowly, might well block, and certainly won't grow as a writer. In line with these concerns, how have we taught our students to respond to mistakes—not just to editing errors, but to the kinds of stylistic and rhetorical blunders that inevitably result from trying the difficult? Anna Brito, the scientist in *An Imagined World*, says, "To be frightened of making mistakes is to be in prison."[13] Writers grow by trying the new. And new conceptual constraints, new stylistic patterns, new audiences bring their own difficulties. If students aren't provided with an appropriate perception of such challenges, they might well be imprisoned by a set of criteria that are appropriate for their more manageable tasks.

In brief, we need to help our students develop the capacity to judge their own work—to judge it appropriately, keeping context and purpose in mind, and to temper their usual judgment as they struggle with the sorts of new tasks that, ultimately, will enhance and develop the criteria by which they will then judge future work.

The Pedagogical Conflict Between Structure and Flexibility

Much of this section stands as a caveat against narrow prescriptions. But it is also true that we cannot teach everything as relative. As I mentioned while discussing the study's implications for a cognitive model of composing, some writing rules are not multioptional. Furthermore, there are times when almost any proposition or strategy might have to be taught rigidly. People often need narrow parameters and rote practice to master a particular technique. In order to balance out a particular student's overly distant, needlessly complicated prose, a teacher might have to have her temporarily write without recourse to the passive voice. To help a writer struggling to find form for his ideas, a tutor might need to present certain simplified discourse patterns, even the five-paragraph form.[14] On the positive side, we often help students grow as writers by forcing them to practice tight stylistic and formal patterns: complex syntactic schemes and rhetorical tropes, and, for those in our creative writing classes, dialogic rhythms and poetic forms. In the beginning of such instruction, a certain cookbookish regularity is necessary.

The question is, then, how do we teachers avoid inculcating the rigid rules and narrow strategies that were constricting the blockers in "Rigid Rules" and the present study? The answers lie in slow weaning, in gradual loosening of structure and expanding of options, in introducing new contexts, in careful monitoring. Let me illustrate with several examples.

The first example deals with the teaching of style. Let us suppose that a teacher decides to expand students' stylistic options by presenting Christensen's generative stylistics. One way to pass the cumulative pattern along is to have students imitate the sentences Christensen singles out,[15] require them to generate sentences that fit the pattern, and then require them to produce such sentences in their own prose. Instruction aimed at building syntactic fluency would usually stop here. But I would suggest further instruction. Once students can demonstrate the pattern and can produce it, the teacher should then turn to discussion of the purpose and appropriateness of the cumulative sentence in various kinds of discourse. Students would examine passages of fictional prose of the kind from which Christensen borrowed his examples. Then students would examine passages of academic exposition or business and technical writing. They would find, as Sandra Thompson nicely demonstrated,[16] that there are relatively few free modifiers in exposition because one of the primary discourse purposes of free modifiers is to describe or, to use her term, "depict." Much more depictive image-evoking goes on in fiction than, say, in reports or analyses. Teachers can then have students examine their own Christensen-like essays and their papers for political science or biology and perform their own tallies of free modifiers. This sort of movement from narrow drill to contextual exploration assures a teacher that though students are mastering certain stylistic strategies, they are also coming to understand that stylistic options aren't executed in a discourse vacuum. Students with such knowledge won't come to think that the best sentence is always the longest or the most modified or the most descriptive.

Another example, one dealing with form. A teacher of a remedial writing course sees that his students are having trouble writing even simple comparisons. The teacher could begin addressing the problem by showing the students a simple compare/contrast pattern (e.g., one in which a similarity is established in one paragraph and a difference is established in the second). Students would use the pattern to write brief compare/contrast papers. Then the teacher offers a second, somewhat more complex pattern (e.g., one in which a similarity and a difference are treated in one paragraph, then a second similarity and difference in a second paragraph). Again, students would use the pattern to write brief compare/contrast papers. Possibly, the teacher could then move to an even more complex pattern (e.g., one in which several similarities and several differences are treated in each of two or three paragraphs). The teacher, in short, would help his students build a repertoire of standard, workaday forms.

Now this could certainly be an appropriate point at which to stop instruction. But, to insure a true understanding of and facility with these patterns, three to four more steps are necessary: (1) Make sure students understand that the patterns they're practicing are just that, patterns—formal conveniences by which information can be laid out in a predictable way. (2) Distinguish between patterns, which are cognitive and rhetorical conveniences for a reader, and strategies, which are procedures the writer uses to explore material. A writer might compare dates, events, or artifacts in a number of unneat, unpatterned ways when she is thinking through her paper, but that freewheeling exploration is not accessible to a reader of school papers, so other—more orderly—structuring is necessary. And, then, there are also instances when discourse patterns can be presented as both structures and strategies, as ways of exploring information as well as ways of presenting it. (3) Because these patterns are conventions and conveniences, they can be reconsidered. If while writing up his ideas, a student thinks of new ideas that won't fit, say, the simple one-similarity, one-paragraph model he's using, then he should modify or even discard his model. His teacher or tutor can help him with this recasting. (4) If enough time remains in the quarter or semester, the teacher should provide opportunities for students to use the pattern(s) in a variety of discourse situations and purposes. For example, students could rely on comparing and contrasting to write a typical social science extended definition; they could also use a simple compare/contrast pattern to set down pros and cons of a decision in a letter to their school's chancellor, and so on. These writing tasks would allow students to see, once again, how even circumscribed language patterns can be incorporated into a variety of discourse needs. So, while it might be necessary to begin teaching a pattern in a somewhat narrow way, the teacher can slowly expand the shapes and uses the pattern can take.

The two examples come from the classroom and extend over time. When the teacher or tutor works with a student or set of students for so long a time, a rich context for rules, patterns, and strategies can be established, and the understanding of that context can be gauged via assignments, student comments, and teacher observation. Unfortunately, not all writing instruction is afforded so much time or occurs in so neat and sequential a fashion. Often the teacher or tutor during conference notices a particular problem, discusses it, has the student carry out a few on-the-spot exercises, and the clock runs out. My advice here would be, first, that the teacher or tutor condense and provide with illustration, if possible, the sort of discussion of context and purpose that has characterized this section. Second, the teacher or tutor should keep a record of the problems discussed with a student. Teachers' files of papers can provide such a record; tutors most likely need to keep a log or journal. The teacher or tutor should periodically review a student's record and test the understanding of solutions to problems discussed during previous sessions. Donald Wasson, of UCLA's AAP Tutorial Center, provided me with a striking example of why such periodic checks are necessary. Reading a student's paper, he saw the sort of fragment the young man used to make but no longer did: "'The reason,' my mother told me when I was growing up, 'if Jesus had not died for us we would not be here today.'" Donald had the good sense not to automatically launch into drills on the fragment but, instead, to ask the student about the construction of the sentence. The student explained that he originally used "Because" rather than "The reason" but remembered that Donald had once told him "'because' causes fragments." The statement was probably misinterpreted or remembered out of context, or perhaps Donald blurted it out in exasperation, but it stands as a dramatic prod to all of us to make sure our advice is appropriately stated—cautious, contextual, and very clear—and to make sure to circle back to old problems. It also reminds us to ask questions—the diagnosing of process I began this section with—before we begin to tell students how to do what we assume they can't do.

Afterword: Areas for Further Investigation

IT IS A CLICHÉ TO SAY A STUDY RAISES MORE QUESTIONS THAN IT answers, but in the present case the cliché is all too appropriate. The fact that writer's block is so broad and unstudied a problem and the fact that the present study, of necessity, is limited to the cognitive dimension of the problem means that a good deal more about stymied composing needs to be discussed and explored. At least six general areas warrant further study.

The Relation of Blocking to Discourse Mode and Audience

The current study involved one discourse mode and one kind of audience: academic exposition written for academic readers. Would blocking or fluency vary, however, as the writer moved outward from, to use James Britton's model, expressive discourse to transactional discourse or, in the other direction, toward poetic discourse?[1] Expressed within another framework, would blocking or fluency be affected as the writer moved along James Moffett's twin continua: I/it (ranging from very personal to impersonal involvement in the topic) and I/you (ranging from intimate to distant connection with audience)?[2] More specifically, would the kinds, numbers, and ratios of rules, plans, assumptions, evaluations, etc., change as discourse and audience changed? Is writer's block state-specific rather than a pervasive trait?

The Relation of Blocking to Situational Context

Tillie Olsen has argued that stymied fluency could well have its origin in a writer's social milieu.[3] Following Olsen's lead, the sociopolitical variables of a student's writing environment should be examined. Would the number, kind, and ratio of composing subprocesses and behaviors vary as the writer moved from a school to a more unstructured and/or more intimate setting? How related are the enactment of these subprocesses (especially rules) to the students' perceptions of the nature and demands of the academic setting? Within the school environment, would variation in teaching style affect blocking? Would blocking correlate with the sociometrically determined position of students in classes; with students' perceptions of how seriously their written expression is taken; with ethnic and social class background?

Temporal Constraints and the Function of the Deadline

The temporal constraints of the present study were partially the result of technological limitations but served the purpose of enhancing the simulation of a school writing environment. But how would high-blockers perform if they had more time to reread, prewrite, and plan, and more time to revise? Would writers like Liz eventually become unstuck?

Of particular interest, given the cases of the three high-blockers, Terryl, Stephanie, and Debbie, is the deadline. While some writers in some situations are negatively affected by deadlines, others (like these three students) are impelled toward the page for one or more of the following related reasons: (1) Uncertainties about skill and fears of evaluation are swept aside (perhaps by some higher-order rule) as the student is focused on the task. (2) Rumination, playful reflection, the weighing of alternatives are cut short. It is, after all, easier to think about writing than it is to write. The deadline channels thinking. (3) Clear temporal boundaries are established, making the task seem more manageable. (4) In line with the classical Yerkes-Dodson law that moderate anxiety is motivating,[4] the deadline could raise a writer's anxiety enough to spark fluency. It would be instructive to explore the role deadlines play in different tasks in different modes for different audiences. Does, for example, the deadline spark the production of expository/transactional discourse but stymie poetic discourse? Does the deadline become less beneficial as discourse becomes more personal and/or more intimately connected to audience?

Cataloguing Composing Subprocesses and Exploring the Internalization of Particular Subprocesses

"Rigid Rules," the present study, and Muriel Harris' compilation of contradictory rules voiced by students[5] suggest that there are myriad rules, planning strategies, assumptions, and evaluative criteria used by student writers. Some aid composing, some limit it. The more writing teachers knew about these rules, plans, etc., the better diagnosticians of certain kinds of writing problems they would be. From open-ended questionnaires, post-hoc interviews, and speaking-aloud and stimulated-recall protocols, researchers could construct catalogues of specific manifestations of composing subprocesses. The sources of these rules, plans, etc., would also be important to know—not only to help remedy certain writing problems but also to gain insight into the contexts in which students learn to write. In addition to the above-mentioned methods of gaining information from students themselves, researchers could analyze writing textbooks to uncover the rules, assumptions, and conceptualizations of composing explicitly or implicitly presented there. Researchers could also conduct ethnographic investigations of student writing environments to find out more about the way rules and planning strategies are taught.

Finally, valuable information on how rules are internalized, modified, and enacted could be gained from pre-post studies similar to standard intervention experiments in which students are tested, taught a method, and tested again. This time, though, the focus and intent would be different. Students would be given instruction in, say, the use of certain rhetorical devices. They would then be post-tested, but, also, their composing processes would be examined via post-hoc interviews or speaking-aloud or stimulated-recall analyses. These investigations could provide some insight into the ways that what is taught is variously processed, made one's own, and employed. Manipulating treatment groups so that the rhetorical devices are taught in narrow fashion or in relation to audience and purpose could provide insight on the development of rigid or flexible rules.

The Relation of Cognitive Styles and Personality Characteristics to Blocking

Several case studies in "The Cognitive Dimension of Writer's Block" (those of Terryl and Gary) suggest a relationship between composing styles and blocking. The case study of Glenn (and of Stephanie in "The Cognitive Dimension of Writer's Block") further suggests that personality characteristics could be related to proficient or limited composing.[6] However, the present study did not involve the sort of testing and extended clinical interviews that would be necessary to diagnose cognitive style or dimensions of personality. As for precedent, my colleague Marcella Graffin is currently engaged in a study of the relation of field-dependent and field-independent cognitive styles to composing, but, to date, no such work has been completed. Sharon Pianko relied on George Kelly's personal construct theory of personality to explore her writers' perceptions of the world.[7] The present study sought explanations for composing behaviors in the writers' cognitive domain: rules, planning strategies, attitudes, and, on a higher level, executive strategies and assumptions. But more fundamental and pervasive styles and predilections could exist; if the reality of these could be demonstrated and their clear relation to composing shown, then the present study could be thought of as revealing a cognitive typology of deep and comprehensive processes and orientations.

The Relation of Blocking and Writing Experience

It was a bit surprising to find that the three students in the study who had the most writing experience and voiced some of the most personal attachments to writing were also high-blockers. The cases of these three (Liz, Terryl, Ruth), all of whom are upper-division

English majors, raise the possibility that as writers develop (at least within the school setting) they can block more. Five reasons for the relation of blocking and experience are possible: (1) The more a student gets involved in writing, the more important it is, the more it reflects her intelligence and values. With this involvement comes a potential increase in anxiety. (2) Desiring growth, the writer continues to challenge himself—continues to face or invent assignments that test, for example, his existing strategies for complexity. He does not rely on the easy approach, the obvious compositional solution, the already mastered pattern. (3) The writer increasingly views writing as poetic discourse, in Britton's sense.[8] Writing becomes more a process with its own justification; text becomes more an object to be refined. This poetic involvement yields felicitous prose but can also result in premature editing. (4) As writers read about other writers, they begin to adopt certain assumptions (e.g., romantic inspiration notions), some of which might mislead. These misleading assumptions lead students to write as they think they ought to rather than as they best can. (5) English departments are at fault. They perhaps instill innumerable rules, assumptions, and criteria—some arbitrary, some rigid, some contradictory. And departments might champion too strongly the literary quip, the grand phrase, narrowing all discourse to variations of poetic discourse.

The present study has defined writer's block as a problem, has, from a pragmatic perspective, viewed restricted fluency as a liability in the school setting. Considering the cases of Liz and Gary, it would be hard to deny the appropriateness of this pragmatic perspective. But the above discussion of experience and blocking suggests that, in some cases, writer's block might be an inevitable part of compositional growth. Britton et al. have noted that "difficulties may actually increase as the writer becomes more proficient."[9] And, perhaps, as the writer becomes more proficient, writing begins to mean more and involve more risks, new structural problems are faced for which new strategies must be learned, the surface of language gains increasing importance, and new syntactic patterns and semantic textures are attempted. Blocking can result. Longitudinal studies of writers would shed light here, could explore the possibility that some blocking might be inevitable as yet greater and more skilled fluency is sought.

Appendixes
Notes

Appendix A
Writer's Block Questionnaire

BELOW ARE 24 STATEMENTS ABOUT WHAT PEOPLE DO OR HOW they feel when they write. Under each is a five-point scale describing degrees of agreement or disagreement with the statement. We would like you to fill in the dot under the degree of agreement or disagreement that best describes your own writing behavior. For example, if the statement reads:

Like Hemingway, I write standing up.

and if you rarely or never write standing up, you should respond in the following way:

THIS DESCRIBES
WHAT I DO OR
HOW I FEEL:

ALMOST ALWAYS (90 to 100% of the time)	OFTEN (75% of the time)	SOMETIMES (50% of the time)	OCCASIONALLY (25% of the time)	ALMOST NEVER (0 to 10% of the time)
○	○	○	○	●

If another statement reads:

I write with #2 pencils.

and if you sometimes do (that is, not always and not rarely but about half the time), you should respond:

THIS DESCRIBES
WHAT I DO OR
HOW I FEEL:

ALMOST ALWAYS (90 to 100% of the time)	OFTEN (75% of the time)	SOMETIMES (50% of the time)	OCCASIONALLY (25% of the time)	ALMOST NEVER (0 to 10% of the time)
○	○	●	○	○

This questionnaire requires that you reflect on your writing behavior. Some items will be easy to answer, but others might be a little difficult because you'll have to analyze what you do by habit. It would probably be best to recall exactly what you did when you wrote a recent paper. This way you can *report what you actually do, not what you wish you could do*. Obviously, you will not be graded on this. Therefore, you can feel free to candidly report what you do and feel when you write. Again, don't report what you would like to do and feel but what you *actually* do and feel. For that fact, as you work through the questionnaire you might realize that an earlier response wasn't right. If that happens, it is OK to go back and change your answer to make it more accurate.

1) Even though it is difficult at times, I enjoy writing.

THIS DESCRIBES
WHAT I DO OR
HOW I FEEL:

ALMOST ALWAYS (90 to 100% of the time)	OFTEN (75% of the time)	SOMETIMES (50% of the time)	OCCASIONALLY (25% of the time)	ALMOST NEVER (0 to 10% of the time)
O	O	O	O	O

2) I've seen some really good writing, and my writing doesn't match up to it.

ALMOST ALWAYS	OFTEN	SOMETIMES	OCCASIONALLY	ALMOST NEVER
O	O	O	O	O

3) My first paragraph has to be perfect before I'll go on.

ALMOST ALWAYS	OFTEN	SOMETIMES	OCCASIONALLY	ALMOST NEVER
O	O	O	O	O

4) I have to hand in assignments late because I can't get the words on paper.

ALMOST ALWAYS	OFTEN	SOMETIMES	OCCASIONALLY	ALMOST NEVER
O	O	O	O	O

5) It is hard for me to write on topics that could be written about from a number of angles.

ALMOST ALWAYS	OFTEN	SOMETIMES	OCCASIONALLY	ALMOST NEVER
O	O	O	O	O

6) I like having the opportunity to express my ideas in writing.

ALMOST ALWAYS	OFTEN	SOMETIMES	OCCASIONALLY	ALMOST NEVER
O	O	O	O	O

7) There are times when I sit at my desk for hours, unable to write a thing.

ALMOST ALWAYS	OFTEN	SOMETIMES	OCCASIONALLY	ALMOST NEVER
O	O	O	O	O

8) I'll wait until I've found just the right phrase.

ALMOST ALWAYS   OFTEN   SOMETIMES   OCCASIONALLY   ALMOST NEVER
        ○   ○   ○   ○   ○

9) While writing a paper, I'll hit places that keep me stuck for an hour or more.

ALMOST ALWAYS   OFTEN   SOMETIMES   OCCASIONALLY   ALMOST NEVER
        ○   ○   ○   ○   ○

10) My teachers are familiar with so much good writing that my writing must look bad by comparison.

ALMOST ALWAYS   OFTEN   SOMETIMES   OCCASIONALLY   ALMOST NEVER
        ○   ○   ○   ○   ○

11) I have trouble figuring out how to write on issues that have many interpretations.

ALMOST ALWAYS   OFTEN   SOMETIMES   OCCASIONALLY   ALMOST NEVER
        ○   ○   ○   ○   ○

12) There are times when it takes me over two hours to write my first paragraph.

ALMOST ALWAYS   OFTEN   SOMETIMES   OCCASIONALLY   ALMOST NEVER
        ○   ○   ○   ○   ○

13) I think my writing is good.

ALMOST ALWAYS   OFTEN   SOMETIMES   OCCASIONALLY   ALMOST NEVER
        ○   ○   ○   ○   ○

14) I run over deadlines because I get stuck while trying to write my paper.

ALMOST ALWAYS   OFTEN   SOMETIMES   OCCASIONALLY   ALMOST NEVER
        ○   ○   ○   ○   ○

15) There are times when I'm not sure how to organize all the information I've gathered for a paper.

ALMOST ALWAYS   OFTEN   SOMETIMES   OCCASIONALLY   ALMOST NEVER
        ○   ○   ○   ○   ○

16) I find myself writing a sentence then erasing it, trying another sentence, then scratching it out. I might do this for some time.

ALMOST ALWAYS   OFTEN   SOMETIMES   OCCASIONALLY   ALMOST NEVER
        ○   ○   ○   ○   ○

17) It is awfully hard for me to get started on a paper.

ALMOST ALWAYS   OFTEN   SOMETIMES   OCCASIONALLY   ALMOST NEVER
        ○   ○   ○   ○   ○

18) Each sentence I write has to be just right before I'll go on to the next sentence.

ALMOST ALWAYS   OFTEN   SOMETIMES   OCCASIONALLY   ALMOST NEVER
        ○   ○   ○   ○   ○

19) I find it difficult to write essays on books and articles that are very complex.

ALMOST ALWAYS	OFTEN	SOMETIMES	OCCASIONALLY	ALMOST NEVER
○	○	○	○	○

20) I think of my instructors reacting to my writing in a positive way.

ALMOST ALWAYS	OFTEN	SOMETIMES	OCCASIONALLY	ALMOST NEVER
○	○	○	○	○

21) Writing is a very unpleasant experience for me.

ALMOST ALWAYS	OFTEN	SOMETIMES	OCCASIONALLY	ALMOST NEVER
○	○	○	○	○

22) There are times when I find it hard to write what I mean.

ALMOST ALWAYS	OFTEN	SOMETIMES	OCCASIONALLY	ALMOST NEVER
○	○	○	○	○

23) I have trouble with writing assignments that ask me to compare and contrast or analyze.

ALMOST ALWAYS	OFTEN	SOMETIMES	OCCASIONALLY	ALMOST NEVER
○	○	○	○	○

24) Some people experience periods when, no matter how hard they try, they can produce little, if any, writing. When these periods last for a considerable amount of time, we say the person has a writing block. Estimate how often you experience writer's block.

ALMOST ALWAYS	OFTEN	SOMETIMES	OCCASIONALLY	ALMOST NEVER
○	○	○	○	○

Appendix B
Results of Statistical Analyses of Writer's Block Questionnaire

Interitem Correlations for the Blocking Subscale

Item	7	9	12	16	17	22	24
7	1.00						
9	.56	1.00					
12	.48	.63	1.00				
16	.36	.47	.48	1.00			
17	.57	.43	.41	.39	1.00		
22	.61	.39	.39	.31	.54	1.00	
24	.42	.28	.34	.32	.47	.47	1.00

Alpha: .85   Interitem Mean: .44

Corrected Item-Total Correlations for the Blocking Subscale

Item	7	9	12	16	17	22	24
	.69	.64	.63	.52	.64	.62	.51

Interitem Correlations for the Lateness Subscale

Item	4	14
4	1.00	
14	.77	1.00

Alpha: .86   Interitem Mean: .77

The corrected Item-Total Correlation for the Lateness Subscale was .77

Interitem Correlations for the Premature Editing Subscale

Item	3	8	18
3	1.00		
8	.41	1.00	
18	.45	.53	1.00

Alpha: .71   Interitem Mean: .46

Corrected Item-Total Correlations for the Premature Editing Subscale

Item	3	8	18
	.49	.54	.58

Interitem Correlations for the Strategies for Complexity Subscale

Item	5	11	15	19	23
5	1.00				
11	.58	1.00			
15	.31	.42	1.00		
19	.37	.47	.38	1.00	
23	.42	.46	.42	.46	1.00

Alpha: .79   Interitem Mean: .43

Corrected Item-Total Correlations for the Strategies for Complexity Subscale

Item	5	11	15	19	23
	.56	.65	.50	.55	.58

Interitem Correlations for the Attitudes Subscale

Item	1	2(R)*	6	10(R)	13	20	21(R)
1	1.00						
2(R)	.20	1.00					
6	.77	.27	1.00				
10(R)	.26	.43	.29	1.00			
13	.48	.45	.52	.54	1.00		
20	.42	.36	.36	.47	.48	1.00	
21(R)	.67	.15	.52	.32	.44	.41	1.00

Alpha: .84   Interitem Mean: .42

*For the statistical analysis, we reversed the direction of three of the items.

Corrected Item-Total Correlations for the Attitudes Subscale

Item	1	2(R)	6	10(R)	13	20	21(R)
	.67	.41†	.66	.51	.69	.57	.60

†According to these statistics, item 2 is not as solid an item as the others in the subscale. I'd press to keep the item, however, because of its conceptual importance to the subscale, because it does hold moderate correlations with three of the other items, and because deleting it would not raise the alpha appreciably.

Correlation Coefficients for Questionnaire Subscales

	Blocking	Lateness	Editing	Complexity	Attitudes
Blocking	1.00				
Lateness	.37	1.00			
Editing	.37	.11	1.00		
Complexity	.59	.23	.12	1.00	
Attitudes	.44	.17	.06	.47*	1.00

*This is the only moderate correlation among the Lateness, Editing, Complexity, and Attitudes subscales. For a discussion of this unexpected correlation, see pp. 124–25.

Blocking as a Function of Subscales Lateness Through Attitudes

	Multiple Correlation	Correlation Squared	B	Beta
Complexity	.59	.35	.604	.416
Lateness	.66	.44	.618	.290
Editing	.70	.49	.742	.198
Attitudes	.72	.52	.205	.192

Appendix C
Assignment Materials for
Stimulated-Recall Study

Instructions

1. Read the case history of Angelo Cacci (it's attached to this sheet) and the quotation from Karl Jaspers printed below.
2. Write an essay in which you discuss Angelo Cacci's situation in terms of the quotation from Jaspers. That is, does Jaspers' passage shed any light on Angelo's situation? If it does, explain how. If it doesn't, explain that as well. Supply evidence from the case history and the quotation to support your assertions.

It has been said that in modern times man has been shuffled together with other men like a grain of sand. He is an element of an apparatus in which he occupies now one location, now another, . . . He has occupation, indeed, but his life has no continuity. What he does is done to good purpose, but is then finished once and for all. The task may be repeated after the same fashion many times, but it cannot be repeated in such an intimate way as to become, one might say, part of the personality of the doer; it does not lead to an expansion of the selfhood . . . Love for things and human beings wanes and disappears. The machine-made products vanish from sight as soon as they are made and consumed; all that remains in view is the machinery by which new commodities are being made. The worker at the machine, concentrating upon immediate aims, has no time or inclination left for the contemplation of life as a whole.

The Case of Angelo Cacci

A young man visited a local counseling center because he was feeling "very down in the dumps." Angelo Cacci was 32 years old, lived alone, and was employed as a clerk in a large insurance company. The counselor noted that Angelo was fairly good looking, clean-shaven, and dressed nicely, though not expensively. He spoke articulately, though not with any particular flair; however, the lack of emphasis in his speech could have been related to his depression. He seemed to be willing to discuss his history and his feelings.

Angelo stated that he had had passing periods of the "blues" before, but that his present feelings of depression were more severe. Several months earlier, Angelo had broken up with his girl friend. "It just wasn't working out," he explained. "We used to go out—go to the park, a ball game, the movies—but after a while it fizzled. I just didn't feel that much for her any more." He added that a similar event had occurred with a different woman five years earlier.

Angelo talked a great deal about his past. He came from an Italian, working-class family. He has a brother and sister but doesn't see either one any longer. His brother was transferred to another large city because the automotive industry was booming there. His sister moved out west after she got married. When Angelo was younger, the Cacci family lived in a predominately Italian neighborhood. Both of the paternal grandparents died when Angelo was quite young. Still, some of Angelo's fondest memories were of his grandfather. The old man used to take him fishing outside the city. Angelo's father, on the other hand, didn't have much time for his children. Mr. Cacci supported the family as a dockworker, but he left when Angelo was 11. After the separation, Mrs. Cacci got a job in a clock factory, and she has worked there ever since.

Angelo explained that his childhood was a very unhappy period. His father was seldom home, and when he was present, he was constantly fighting with Mrs. Cacci. Mrs. Cacci usually became sullen and withdrawn after an argument, refused to speak to her husband, and became uncommunicative with her children. Angelo remembered that many times as a child he was puzzled because it seemed that his mother was angry with him too. Sometimes after an argument, Mrs. Cacci told her children that she ruined her life by marrying a "truckdriver." Angelo went on, explaining that his mother rarely smiled or laughed and did not converse very much with the children. When she came home from work she would usually put on her robe, cook dinner, and spend the evening watching television. This pattern continued well into Angelo's young adulthood.

After high school, Angelo went into the Army where he developed good typing, clerical, and basic accounting skills. He describes the Army as being uneventful. He put in his time and was honorably discharged.

Angelo characterized his job as being, "O.K." "It pays the bills and leaves me a decent amount for entertainment." His particular task is to certify damage claims by checking customer estimates against insurance investigator reports. This provides the company with the information it needs to challenge possibly exaggerated or even fraudulent claims. On an average day, Angelo said he examines and registers twenty to twenty-five estimates and reports. The counselor noted that Angelo's work record must be a good one. He has been with the company for ten years and regularly gets the raises afforded employees in good standing.

The reason for Angelo's visit to the counseling center, his depression, puzzled him. He recounted a dream he has had several times in the last month, wondering if it is connected to his depression. The counselor described the dream in Angelo's case history, but, though she might have offered an interpretation, she didn't write it down. In the dream Angelo and a man from another department in the insurance firm are walking in an open field. Horses are roaming the area as are several large dogs. One of the dogs seems to be injured and limps by Angelo and his friend. A third man appears and begins attending to the dog. Here either the dream fades or Angelo wakes up. Angelo then turned to other aspects of his life, but didn't see any immediate connection between them and his situation. "Sure I broke up with my girl," he speculated, "but I wasn't in love with her. Besides, I've been through this before." As for his job, "like I explained, it's all right. I've got a good record and the pay is satisfactory." As for his mother, "I go to see her now and then. She's still gloomy as always, but I realize there's little I can do about it. She's been that way for a long time."

Appendix D
Analytic Scale for Evaluating the Stimulated-Recall Essays

Punctuation and Spelling   _____ pts. × 1 = _____

3 = Correct use of punctuation marks (i.e., commas, apostro-
        phes, periods, quotation marks, semicolons, colons, etc.).

2.5

2 = A few punctuation errors (i.e., occasional omission or error
        of punctuation). Minor weakness in spelling (e.g., occasional
        misspelling of complex words).

1.5

1 = Major punctuation errors (e.g., difficulty with several
        punctuation marks). Major weakness in spelling; many
        spelling errors.

 .5

0 = Poor punctuation (e.g., absence of punctuation; frequent
        use of wrong punctuation marks). Poor spelling; frequent
        spelling errors.

Grammar   _____ pts. × 1 = _____

3   = Good construction, including proper word order, referents,
        subject-verb agreement, parallel structure, modifier and
        clause placement, etc.

2.5

2 = Minor weaknesses in grammar (e.g., grammatical errors confined to one item; a few grammatical errors; i.e., errors that, in the context of the essay, cause the reader some distraction).

1.5

1 = Major weaknesses in grammar (several and various grammatical errors; i.e., errors that, in the context of the essay, cause the reader significant distraction).

 .5

0 = Poor grammar (i.e., improper word order, dangling/misplaced modifiers, sentence fragments, lack of agreement run-on, etc.).

Thesis and Evidence   _____ pts. × 2 = _____

3 = Thesis is clearly stated and adequately reflects the purpose of the assignment; evidence is relevant and adequately supports the thesis.

2.5

2 = Minor weakness in statement of thesis and/or use of evidence (e.g., thesis is somewhat ambiguous or vague or slightly off the topic; student introduces some irrelevant evidence).

1.5

1 = Major weakness in thesis statement and/or use of evidence (e.g., thesis is ambiguous or very vague or ignores the purpose of the assignment; evidence is scanty or not related to the points under discussion).

 .5

0 = Absence of stated thesis and/or absence of relevant evidence.

Organization and
Development   _____ pts. × 2 = _____

3   = The sequence of ideas (paragraphs) in the paper is clear,
      logical, and complete; paragraphs have topic sentences/tran-
      sitions and are internally coherent.
2.5
2   = Minor weaknesses in overall organization pattern and/or
      paragraph structure (e.g., some irrelevant ideas/paragraphs
      included; some passages or paragraphs make no major
      point).
1.5
1   = Major weaknesses in organization and/or paragraph
      structure (e.g., frequent digressions; few transitions; serious
      omissions or underdevelopment).
 .5
0   = Lack of overall organization and/or absence of coherent
      paragraphs (e.g., no explicit relationships among ideas in
      the paper; many one-sentence paragraphs, etc.).

Sentence Style   _____ pts. × 2 = _____

3   = Sentence length is varied. Prose has some rhythm.
2.5
2   = Sentence length is relatively varied. Prose tends toward a
      rhythm, though that rhythm is not fully realized.
1.5
1   = Extensive reliance on one type of sentence—simple or
      complex. Prose displays little or no rhythm.
 .5
0   = Complete lack of sentence variety. Prose is monotonous,
      displays no rhythm.

Diction   _____ pts. × 2 = _____

3   = Word choice is logical (appropriate), varied, and precise.
      Figurative language, if present, is fresh.

2.5
2   = Minor weaknesses in word choice and variation (e.g., some words/expressions are used inappropriately/repetitively). Figurative language, if present, is relatively fresh.
1.5
1   = Major weaknesses in word-choice and variation (e.g., frequent use of ambiguous or inappropriate words). Figurative language, if present, is ordinary.
 .5
0   = Poor and unvaried diction (e.g., inappropriate selection of words/idioms and/or reliance on simple words characterize the essay). Figurative language, if present, is clichéd or muddled.

Quality of Analysis   _____ pts. × 3 = _____

3   = The essay displays multiple ideas that are insightful, more than ordinary.
2.5
2   = The essay displays one idea that is very insightful or more than one idea that is fairly insightful.
1.5
1   = The essay displays a single idea that is obvious but is pushed beyond the most simple of interpretations.
 .5
0   = The essay displays idea(s) that are simple and obvious.

General principle for defining 4-point scales:
3 = Very good, satisfies all requirements
2 = Good, satisfies most requirements (some deficiencies)
1 = Fair, satisfies few requirements (many deficiencies)
0 = Poor, deficient in all respects

COLLEGE OF THE SEQUOIAS
LIBRARY

Notes

1. Introduction

1. See, for example, the following news articles: "Careers: Axing Writer's Block," *Washington Post*, 12 June 1980, p. D-5; "In California: Confronting the Empty Page," *Time*, 14 July 1980, 8; "Breaking Through Writer's Block," Los Angeles *Times*, 10 Oct. 1980, pt. 5, p. 23.

2. Morris Holland, "The State of the Art: The Psychology of Writing" (Paper presented at the Inland Area Writing Project's Summer Writing Conference, Univ. of California at Riverside, July 1980).

3. Mike Rose, "Rigid Rules, Inflexible Plans, and the Stifling of Language: A Cognitivist Analysis of Writer's Block," *College Composition and Communication* 31 (1980): 389–401.

4. Mina P. Shaughnessy, *Errors and Expectations* (New York: Oxford Univ. Pr., 1977); Sondra Perl, "'Five Writers Writing': Case Studies of the Composing Processes of Unskilled College Writers" (Ph.D. diss., New York Univ., 1978).

5. John A. Daly, "The Effects of Writing Apprehension on Message Encoding," *Journalism Quarterly* 54 (1977): 566–72; John A. Daly, "Writing Apprehension and Writing Competency," *The Journal of Educational Research* 2 (1978): 10–14; John A. Daly, "Writing Apprehension in the Classroom: Teacher Role Expectancies of the Apprehensive Writer," *Research in the Teaching of English* 12 (1978): 37–44; John A. Daly and Michael D. Miller, "The Empirical Development of an Instrument to Measure Writing Apprehension," *Research in the Teaching of English* 9 (1975): 242–49; John A. Daly and Michael D. Miller, "Further Studies on Writing Apprehension: SAT Scores, Success Expectations, Willingness to Take Advanced Courses, and Sex Differences," *Research in the Teaching of English* 9 (1975): 250–56; John A. Daly and

Michael D. Miller, "Apprehension of Writing as a Predictor of Message Intensity," *The Journal of Psychology* 89 (1975): 175–77; and John A. Daly and Wayne Shamo, "Academic Decisions as a Function of Writing Apprehension," *Research in the Teaching of English* 12 (1978): 119–26.

6. Lynn Bloom, "Teaching Anxious Writers: Implications and Applications of Research" (Paper presented at Conference on College Composition and Communication, Minneapolis, Apr. 1979); Lynn Bloom, "The Composing Processes of Anxious and Nonanxious Writers" (Paper presented at the Conference on College Composition and Communication, Washington, DC, Mar. 1980); Lynn Bloom, "The Fear of Writing," *William and Mary Quarterly* (Winter 1980), 25–29.

7. Daly, "Writing Apprehension and Writing Competency."

8. Lawrence Kubie, *Neurotic Distortions of the Creative Process* (New York: Noonday, 1973); Paul Federn, "The Neurotic Style," *Psychoanalytic Quarterly* 31 (1957): 681–89.

9. James Moffett, *Teaching the Universe of Discourse* (Boston: Houghton, 1968).

10. Mike Rose, "Remedial Writing Courses: A Critique and a Proposal," *College English* 45 (1983): 109–28.

11. I'm bringing cognitive and linguistic processes together here not to suggest that they're identical, but to suggest that the abilities to interpret writing tasks, plan for them, and produce and structure language to accommodate them are, *in general*, related and must be considered in a discussion of stymied or fluent composing.

12. M. A. K. Halliday and Ruquaiya Hasan, *Cohesion in English* (London: Longmans, 1976).

13. James W. Ney, "Notes Toward a Psycholinguistic Model of the Writing Process," *Research in the Teaching of English* 8 (1974): 157–69.

14. James A. Schellenberg, *An Introduction to Social Psychology*, 2d ed. (New York: Random, 1974), 151.

15. Daly and Miller, "Further Studies on Writing Apprehension"; Holland, "State of the Art."

16. Bertram Bruce, Allan Collins, and Ann D. Rubin, "A Cognitive Science Approach to Writing" (Paper presented at the NIE Writing Conference, Los Alamitos, CA, June 1977); Ellen Nold, "Revising," in *Writing: The Nature, Development, and Teaching of Written Communication*, ed. Carl H. Frederiksen and J. F. Dominic (Hillsdale, NJ: Erlbaum, in press); Linda S. Flower and John R. Hayes, *A Process Model of Composition*, Technical Report no. 1, Document Design Project, Carnegie-Mellon Univ., May 1979.

17. George A. Miller, Eugene Galanter, and Karl H. Pribram, *Plans and the Structure of Behavior* (New York: Holt, 1960).

18. Barbara Hayes-Roth and Frederick Hayes-Roth, "A Cognitive Model of Planning," *Cognitive Science* 3 (1979): 275–310.

19. Donald M. Murray, "Internal Revision: A Process of Discovery," in *Research on Composing: Points of Departure*, ed. Charles R. Cooper and Lee Odell (Urbana: National Council of Teachers of English, 1978).

20. James Britton, "The Composing Processes and the Functions of Writing," in *Research on Composing: Points of Departure*, ed. Charles R. Cooper and Lee Odell (Urbana: National Council of Teachers of English, 1978).

21. Allen Newell and Herbert A. Simon, *Human Problem Solving* (Englewood Cliffs, NJ: Prentice-Hall, 1972).

22. Jerry Feitelson and Mark Stefik, "A Case Study of the Reasoning in a Genetics Experiment," Heuristic Programming Project, Working Paper 77-18, Department of Computer Science, Stanford Univ., Apr. 1977.

23. However, discussions of the composing process occasionally raise the issue of writer's block. See, for example, Linda S. Flower and John R. Hayes, "Problem Solving and the Cognitive Process of Writing," unpublished manuscript, Carnegie-Mellon Univ., 1977; Sondra Perl and Arthur Egendorf, "The Process of Creative Discovery: Theory, Research, and Implications for Teaching," in *Linguistics, Stylistics, and the Teaching of Composition*, ed. Donald McQuade (Conway, AR: L and S Books, 1979).

24. Tillie Olsen, *Silences* (New York: Dell, 1979).

25. *Writers at Work*, 4 vols., ed. Malcolm Cowley and George Plimpton (New York: Penguin, 1977).

26. Federn, "Neurotic Style."

27. Kubie, *Neurotic Distortions*.

28. Marvin Rosenberg, "Releasing the Creative Imagination," *Journal of Creative Behavior* 10 (1976): 203–9.

29. Edmund Bergler, *The Basic Neurosis* (New York: Grune and Stratton, 1949); Edmund Bergler, "Does 'Writer's Block' Exist?" *American Imago* 7 (1959): 43–54; Edmund Bergler, *The Writer and Psychoanalysis*, 2d ed. (New York: Robert Brunner, 1954); Edmund Bergler, "Unconscious Mechanisms in 'Writer's Block,'" *Psychoanalytic Review* 42 (1955): 160–67.

30. Paul Goodman, "On a Writer's Block," *Complex* 7 (1952): 42–50.

31. The 20 texts follow: W. Royce Adams, *TRRPWR*, 2d ed. (New York: Holt, 1979); Sheridan Baker, *The Complete Stylist and Handbook* (New York: Crowell, 1976); Jim W. Corder, *Contemporary Writing: Process and Practice* (Glenview, IL: Scott, 1979); Gregory Cowan and Elizabeth McPherson, *Plain English Rhetoric and Reader*, 2d ed. (New York:

Random, 1977); Frederick Crews, *The Random House Handbook*, 2d ed. (New York: Random, 1977); Frank J. D'Angelo, *Process and Thought in Composition* (Cambridge: Winthrop, 1975); Mary Ellen Grasso and Margaret Maney, *You Can Write* (Cambridge: Winthrop, 1975); Hans P. Guth, *Words and Ideas—A Handbook for College Writing*, 4th ed. (Belmont, CA: Wadsworth, 1975); Donald Hall, *Writing Well*, 3d ed. (Boston: Little, 1979); Harold J. Janis, *College Writing* (New York: Macmillan, 1977); John Langan, *English Skills* (New York: McGraw, 1977); Ken Macrorie, *Telling Writing*, 2d ed. rev. (Rochelle Park, NJ: Hayden, 1976); Ruth L. Optner, *Writing from the Inside Out* (New York: Harper, 1977); Edgar V. Roberts, *A Practical College Rhetoric* (Cambridge: Winthrop, 1975); William F. Smith and Raymond D. Liedlich, *From Thought to Theme*, 5th ed. (New York: Harcourt, 1977); A. M. Tibbetts and Charlene Tibbetts, *Strategies of Rhetoric*, 3d ed. (Glenview, IL: Scott, 1979); A. D. Van Nostrand et al., *Functional Writing* (Boston: Houghton, 1978); Hulon Willis, *Logic, Language and Composition* (Cambridge: Winthrop, 1975); Anthony C. Winkler and Joe Ray McCuen, *Rhetoric Made Plain*, 2d ed. (New York: Harcourt, 1978); W. Ross Winterowd, *The Contemporary Writer—A Practical Rhetoric* (New York: Harcourt, 1975).

32. Karin Mack and Eric Skjei, *Overcoming Writing Blocks* (Los Angeles: Tarcher, 1979); Joan Minninger, *Free Yourself to Write* (San Francisco: Workshops for Innovative Teaching, 1980).

33. Daly, "Effects of Writing Apprehension"; Daly, "Writing Apprehension and Writing Competency"; Daly, "Writing Apprehension in the Classroom"; Daly and Miller, "Empirical Development of an Instrument"; Daly and Miller, "Further Studies on Writing Apprehension"; Daly and Miller, "Apprehension of Writing as a Predictor"; Daly and Shamo, "Academic Decisions"; Holland, "State of the Art"; L. Bloom, "Teaching Anxious Writers"; L. Bloom, "Composing Processes of Anxious and Nonanxious Writers"; L. Bloom, "Fear of Writing."

34. Daly, "Writing Apprehension in the Classroom," 37.

35. Daly, "Writing Apprehension and Writing Competency," 13.

36. I must apologize for using these stylistically troublesome and personally offensive labels. But every alternative I tried resulted in elaborate language (e.g., "students experiencing a high degree of writer's block vs. students experiencing a low degree of writer's block") which became unwieldy when I had to compare the two groups along a number of criteria. Therefore, I decided to rely on the shorthand "high-blockers" and "low-blockers." The labels are bothersome but at least do not clutter, and, furthermore, they reinforce the important notion that we are dealing with extremes along a continuum.

2. The Study: Questionnaire and Stimulated-Recall Investigation—Procedures and Results

1. Charles R. Cooper and Lee Odell, "Considerations of Sound in the Composing Process of Published Writers," *Research in the Teaching of English* 10 (1976): 103–15.

2. Lee J. Cronbach, *Essentials of Psychological Testing*, 3d ed. (New York: Harper, 1970).

3. Michael Anthony Rose, "The Cognitive Dimension of Writer's Block: An Examination of University Students" (Ph.D. diss., Univ. of California, Los Angeles, 1981).

4. Charles K. Stallard, "Analysis of the Writing Behavior of Good Student Writers," *Research in the Teaching of English* 8 (1974): 208–18; Sharon Pianko, "The Composing Acts of College Freshman Writers: A Description" (Ph.D. diss., Rutgers Univ., 1977); Nancy I. Sommers, "Revision in the Composing Process: A Case Study of College Freshmen and Experienced Adult Writers" (Ph.D. diss., Boston Univ., 1978).

5. Janet Emig, *The Composing Processes of Twelfth Graders* (Urbana: National Council of Teachers of English, 1971); Terry Mischel, "A Case Study of a Twelfth-Grade Writer," *Research in the Teaching of English* 8 (1974): 303–14; Sondra Perl, "'Five Writers Writing'"; Flower and Hayes, *A Process Model*.

6. Ann Matsuhashi, "Producing Written Discourse: A Theory-based Description of the Temporal Characteristics of Three Discourse Types from Four Competent Grade 12 Writers" (Ph.D. diss., State Univ. of New York at Buffalo, 1979).

7. Cooper and Odell, "Considerations of Sound in the Composing Process."

8. Marshall Atlas, "A Brief Overview of Research Methods for the Writing Researcher," unpublished paper, Carnegie-Mellon Univ., n.d.

9. William Styron, interview reported in *Writers at Work*, 1st ser., ed. Malcolm Cowley (New York: Penguin, 1977).

10. Benjamin S. Bloom, "The Thought Processes of Students in Discussion," in *Accent on Teaching: Experiments in General Education*, ed. Samuel J. French (New York: Harper, 1954), 25.

11. Bloom, "Thought Processes of Students," 25.

12. Norman Kagan, David R. Krathwohl, and Ralph Miller, "Stimulated Recall in Therapy Using Videotape—A Case Study," *Journal of Counseling Psychology* 10 (1963): 237–43.

13. I defined an "extreme" subscale score as one that is one standard deviation or more above or below the average score (of all students) on that subscale. The standard deviation of a set of scores is a measure of the

spread of scores around the average (mean) score. My rationale for using one standard deviation to identify "high" and "low" scores went as follows: If we can assume that the distribution of the subscales' scores around their respective means is normal, then we know that if we choose students one standard deviation above and one standard deviation below the mean, we will be dealing with the top 14 percent and bottom 14 percent of all students who responded to that subscale.

I recruited students in the following way. Twenty-two students fell one standard deviation above the Blocking mean (i.e., were high-blockers), and they ranged from category one through eight in English experience. Of the 22, 20 also scored one standard deviation or more above a process and/or attitude subscale. (I would select one of the remaining two students for the study to determine why her process and/or attitude subscale scores were not extreme. This was Liz.) I chose six high-blockers. No student who was one standard deviation below the Blocking mean (i.e., was a low-blocker) also scored one standard deviation below a process and/or attitude subscale. I therefore lowered the cutting edge from one to .8 of a standard deviation, and 18 students were identified. (Their standard deviations turned out to be very close to one—e.g., .95, .96, .91.) I chose four. Their English experience ranged from categories one to six.

Let me now explain how I determined English experience. The procedure, I'll admit, was much less rigorous than that used to determine high- and low-blockers, but the problem was, in many ways, a messier one. Certainly courses other than English require writing. But the consistency and amount from department to department and professor to professor over the one to four years the 351 students span would be virtually impossible to estimate. Therefore, I decided to determine experience by criteria I could set with some certainty:

1. Subject A (remedial English) and Advanced Placement (composition requirement fulfilled by examination) status—these designations, one hopes, imply something about the experience and skills students possess when they enter UCLA.

2. Writing courses completed.

3. English and Humanities courses completed—except those which do not regularly require papers and essay examinations.

Student data sheets were examined with these criteria in mind. Eight categories emerged:

Category 1: Held for Subject A and not yet completed Composition
Category 2: Held for and completed Subject A and Composition
Category 3: Not held for Subject A but not yet completed Composition
Category 4: Not held for Subject A and completed Composition
Category 5: Advanced Placement but no further English courses taken

Category 6: Held for and completed Subject A and Composition and has taken further English courses

Category 7: Not held for Subject A, completed Composition and has taken further English courses

Category 8: Advanced Placement and further English courses taken

I checked the transcripts of the 10 students chosen for the stimulated-recall study to verify the accuracy of student self-reports. All reports were accurate.

14. Rose, "Remedial Writing Courses."

15. Sharon Crowley, "Components of the Composing Process," *College Composition and Communication* 28 (1977): 176–79.

16. "The broad objectives of the study should be made known to the subject to reduce the danger of his constructing his own theory about the researcher's intentions and so distorting data." N. B. Tuckwell, *Stimulated Recall: Theoretical Perspectives and Practical and Technical Considerations*, Technical Report 8-2-3, Centre for Research in Teaching, Univ. of Alberta, 1980, 7.

17. Richard E. Nisbett and Timothy DeCamp Wilson, "Telling More Than We Can Know: Verbal Reports on Mental Processes," *Psychological Review* 84 (1977): 231–59.

18. K. Anders Ericsson and Herbert Simon, "Verbal Reports as Data," *Psychological Review* 87 (1980): 215–51.

19. A measure of inter-rater reliability is simply a measure of the consistency among the scores of independent raters. The coefficient ranges from 0 to 1.0.

20. D. Gordon Rohman, "Pre-writing: The Stage of Discovery in the Writing Process," *College Composition and Communication* 16 (1965): 106–12.

21. Flower and Hayes, *A Process Model*.

22. Pianko, "Composing Acts of College Freshman Writers," 277.

23. Perl, "'Five Writers Writing.'"

24. Rose, "Cognitive Dimension of Writer's Block."

25. See n. 19 for an explanation of inter-rater reliability.

26. Independent scores as well as summary commentaries for all essays can be found in "Cognitive Dimension of Writer's Block."

3. Case Studies of Two Students

1. See n. 13, chap. 2, for a definition of standard deviation and a rationale for using one standard deviation above or below the mean as the criterion for selecting students for the stimulated-recall study.

2. Linda Flower, *Problem Solving Strategies for Writing* (New York: Harcourt, 1981).

3. Michael Polanyi, *Personal Knowledge* (Chicago: Univ. of Chicago Pr., 1962).

4. Linda Flower and John R. Hayes, "The Cognition of Discovery: Defining a Rhetorical Problem," *College Composition and Communication* 31 (1980): 21–32.

5. Emig, *Composing Processes of Twelfth Graders.*

6. Gary Sloan, "Predilections for Plethoric Prose," *College English* 39 (1978): 860–65; Rosemary L. Hake and Joseph M. Williams, "Style and Its Consequences: Do as I Do, Not as I Say," *College English* 43 (1981): 433–51.

7. Earlier Glenn said that after he pours an idea out onto paper he can "go back and worry about whether its grammatically perfect or not," yet here he says he "almost never proofread(s) a paper." (And, in fact, he did not methodically proofread the present essay.) These two statements might not be contradictory. Glenn could mean that after dashing out a particular sentence, he'll tend to quickly look back over it and clean it up (the tape displayed some behavior of this sort), but that after an essay is done, he rarely rereads the entire text for error. Yet, there could be an element of contradiction here, and—major concern— these comments provide illustration of the kind of broad, general statements I caution about while discussing methodology in chap. 2. Therefore, I don't make too much of them in my analysis of the protocol.

8. Perl, "'Five Writers Writing.'"

9. Rose, "Rigid Rules."

10. Before we label this statement immature or complacent, we should consider a further statement, one by William Stafford: "There are never mornings when I can't write. I think there are never mornings that anybody 'can't write.' I think that anybody could write if he would have standards as low as mine." *Writing the Australian Crawl* (Ann Arbor: Univ. of Michigan Pr., 1978), 104. There are times when settling for second-best might aid more than limit our composing.

4. Conclusion

1. Perl, "'Five Writers Writing.'"

2. Correlations between the Premature Editing subscale and pilot items dealing with planning styles (e.g., "I have a basic idea of how to write a paper. I usually follow it rather than writing down an outline.") ranged from .11 to .21. The planning items were included to test other hypotheses and were not included in the final questionnaire.

3. Flower and Hayes, *A Process Model.*

4. See, for example, Herman A. Witkin et al., "Field-dependent and

Field-independent Cognitive Styles and Their Educational Implications," *Review of Educational Research* 47 (1977): 1–64; Jerome Kagan, "Impulsive and Reflective Children: Significance of the Conceptual Tempo," in *Learning and the Educational Process*, ed. John D. Krumboltz (Chicago: Rand, 1965).

5. Daly and Miller, "Empirical Development of an Instrument," 246.

6. Mike Rose, "Sophisticated, Ineffective Books—The Dismantling of Process in Composition Texts," *College Composition and Communication* 32 (1981): 65–74; Mike Rose, "Speculations on Process Knowledge and the Textbook's Static Page," *College Composition and Communication*, in press; Rose, "Remedial Writing Courses."

7. Mary Vaiana Taylor, "The Folklore of Usage," *College English* 35 (1974): 756–68.

8. Rose, "Speculations on Process Knowledge."

9. See, for example, Sandra A. Thompson, "The Passive in English: A Discourse Perspective," unpublished paper, Department of Linguistics, University of California, Los Angeles; Elizabeth Ann Turner and Ragnar Rommetveit, "Focus of Attention in Recall of Active and Passive Sentences," *Journal of Verbal Learning and Verbal Behavior* 7 (1968): 543; Richard A. Lanham, *Style: An Anti-textbook* (New Haven: Yale Univ. Pr., 1974); Richard Ohmann, "Use Definite, Specific, Concrete Language," *College English* 41 (1979): 390–97.

10. Cynthia L. Selfe and Sue Rodi, "An Invention Heuristic for Expressive Writing," *College Composition and Communication* 31 (1980): 169–74; Tommy J. Boley, "A Heuristic for Persuasion," *College Composition and Communication* 30 (1979): 187–91; Fred R. Pfister and Joanne F. Petrick, "A Heuristic Model for Creating a Writer's Audience," *College Composition and Communication* 31 (1980): 213–20.

11. Rose, "Rigid Rules," 397.

12. Rose, "Remedial Writing Courses," sec. 5.

13. Quoted in June Goodfield, *An Imagined World* (New York: Harper, 1981), 31.

14. See, for example, Arthur Applebee, *Writing in the Secondary School* (Urbana: National Council of Teachers of English, 1981), 82–83.

15. For example, this sentence from Sinclair Lewis: "He dipped his hands in the biochloride solution and shook them, a quick shake, fingers down, like the fingers of the pianist above the keys." Francis Christensen, *Notes Toward a New Rhetoric*, 2d ed. (New York: Harper, 1978).

16. Sandra A. Thompson, "Grammar and Discourse: The English Detached Participial Clause," in *Discourse Approaches to Syntax*, ed. Flora Klein (Norwood, NJ: Ablex, in press).

Afterword

1. James Britton, *Language and Learning* (Harmondsworth, England: Penguin, 1970).
2. Moffett, *Teaching the Universe of Discourse*.
3. Olsen, *Silences*.
4. R. M. Yerkes and J. D. Dodson, "The Relation of Strength to Stimulus to Rigidity of Habit Formation," *Journal of Comparative Neurological Psychology* 18 (1908): 459–82.
5. Rose, "Rigid Rules"; Muriel Harris, "Contradictory Perceptions of Rules for Writing," *College Composition and Communication* 30 (1979): 218–20.
6. See chap. 5, pp. 111–27, 128–41, and 156–69.
7. Pianko, "Composing Acts of College Freshman Writers."
8. Britton, *Language and Learning*.
9. James Britton et al., *The Development of Writing Abilities (11–18)* (London: Macmillan, 1975).

1490